As I Remembered
A Memoir

Stanley S. Chen

iUniverse, Inc.
New York   Bloomington

As I Remembered
A Memoir

iUniverse books may be ordered through booksellers or by contacting:

iUniverse
1663 Liberty Drive
Bloomington, IN 47403
www.iuniverse.com
1-800-Authors (1-800-288-4677)

Because of the dynamic nature of the Internet, any Web addresses or links contained in this book may have changed since publication and may no longer be valid. The views expressed in this work are solely those of the author and do not necessarily reflect the views of the publisher, and the publisher hereby disclaims any responsibility for them.

ISBN: 978-1-4502-3985-1 (pbk)
ISBN: 978-1-4502-3987-5 (cloth)
ISBN: 978-1-4502-3986-8 (ebk)

Printed in the United States of America

iUniverse rev. date: 6/23/10

To my family: my loving wife (a mother and grandmother herself) Nancy; my sons, Hector and Victor; and their loving wives, Jennie and Sally, respectively. My grandchildren, Victoria, Valerie, Samuel, and Sophia. Without them my life would not be complete.

CONTENTS

Prologue xi

Chapter I: During the Sino-Japanese War 1
Chapter II: The Whole Family United 5
Chapter III: Life Under the Communist Government 11
Chapter IV: Journey to Taiwan 19
Chapter V: Junior High School and College 24
Chapter VI: Met My Sweetheart and Lifetime Companion .. 29
Chapter VII: Military Service 36
Chapter VIII: Preparation for Studying Abroad 44
Chapter IX: Crossing the Pacific Ocean 51
Chapter X: The Ohio University Days 55
Chapter XI: Working for A. O. Smith Corporation
and Marriage 67
Chapter XII: Entering Parenthood 79
Chapter XIII: Doctoral Studies at the University Of
Wisconsin-Madison 84
Chapter XIV: Job Hunting 96
Chapter XV: Teaching at Arizona State University 102
Chapter XVI: Naturalized as an American Citizen 111
Chapter XVII: Visiting Professorship in Taiwan 113
Chapter XVIII: Visiting Professorship in China 122
Chapter XIX: Extracurricular Activities 132
Chapter XX: Our Children 145
Chapter XXI: Retiring From Teaching 159
Chapter XXII: Mother Joining Us Permanently 165
Chapter XXIII: Retirement Years and Reflecting on our Lives . 173

ACKNOWLEDGMENTS

My elder son, Hector, helped me a great deal in editing, making suggestions about certain events, and integrating photographs into the body of the writing. For that I acknowledge his efforts and my appreciation.

PROLOGUE

I did not meet my parents, aside from the early weeks after I was born, until I was eight. I don't think that I ever thought about them or wondered about what they were like while I was being moved about from relative to relative in villages in the county of Haiyen Xian, Zhejiang Province.

Chapter I:

During the Sino-Japanese War

I was born in the morning (according to my mother) on February 24, 1937 (lunar calendar) in Hangzhou, Zhejiang, China. I have always used the western calendar when giving my birthday instead of trying to convert it to the actual Western calendar to avoid the confusing. At the time of my birth, World War II had already started. Japan had invaded Manchuria, but the Sino-Japanese War was not officially declared until sometime in July of that year. China was in turmoil. My father worked for the central government of the Republic of China as a military justice at that time. He was constantly on the move because of his job.

As with my sister, Shiao Hui, born on February 22, 1934, and brother Hsiao (the different spelling was by his own choice) Tsung, born on July 14, 1935, my parents hired a wet nurse for me. After about two weeks, I was sent to live with my uncle (number two in my father's generation of four male children) in a village in Haiyen Xian (Xian means county as in the US), Zhejiang. Later on, I learned that this uncle's wife is also my mother's elder sister. My two elder siblings were living with my maternal grandfather. I did not meet my parents until I was eight, after the war was over.

I did not remember much up till I was about five, when my uncle (I addressed him as Da Bai) died of cholera caught while attending the funeral of my first maternal grandmother, who had died of the same disease. Since Da Yi (my elder aunt) already had a daughter, it would have been extremely difficult for her to raise two children

1

alone. So I was sent to live with my maternal grandfather from here on he is the only grandfather (my paternal grandfather had passed away when my father was fourteen).

I only stayed at my grandfather's for a short while, because my sister and brother rejected me. They had never met me before and always found ways to pick on me. I must have cried a lot, as my grandfather, with agreement from my father's younger brother, sent me to live with his family in another village after the new year, before I turned six. At that time, Uncle already had five kids, so one more did not matter to him. Again I started out being the new kid in the group, the one everybody would pick on. Fortunately, there were two cousins who were younger than I was, and when we got picked on we all cried together. As Uncle was an equal-opportunity punisher he just spanked everyone. The oldest cousin was a boy, about eleven, his face pocked as a result of smallpox. We sometimes deliberately provoked him by calling him "Pock Face." I rarely joined the teasing, for reasons of self-preservation. When Uncle saw Pock Face hitting one of us, the older boy would be the one who ended up punished.

During the short stay at my grandfather's home, I was allowed to join with my sister and brother and a couple of other kids from the same village in receiving instruction from a tutor. It must have been toward the end of the year (around early December 1942), when one of the kids from the village caught meningitis and passed it on to me. I had an extremely high fever and was in and out of consciousness for over twenty-four hours. Fortunately, my aunt had some nursing training and decided my illness was very serious. She convinced Grandfather that I should be taken to the nearest town, Xiashi, by row boat, to be seen by a doctor trained in western medicine. The doctor gave me a shot of penicillin. On the way home, a trip of about four hours, my fever came down and I felt normal again. The next morning I peered out of an upstairs window at the house's central hall. I saw Grandfather was praying to Buddha and deceased ancestors by burning candles and incense. He offered a pig's head and other dishes for my recovery. I felt so moved that my family loved me so much. Later on I learned that the village boy who had the disease at the same time died a day after I went to the doctor.

His family went to the local temple to pray to Buddha, but did not treat him with a penicillin shot.

When I turned six, Uncle let me study in the central hall with the older kids. We were taught by a tutor Uncle had hired because there was no school in the village where we lived. We mostly recited out of some old Chinese book and practiced calligraphy. I remember, before my illness, being able to recite a page after only reading it once, because the words seemed to appear on the wall (I guess I had a photographic memory). I was told how smart I was. After I recovered from the meningitis, I had to read the pages a few times before I could commit the texts to memory.

Life was quite peaceful in the village, although the Sino-Japanese War was raging. Very few Japanese solders ever ventured into our village. China is so vast that there were not enough troops to occupy every city, county, and village. I can only remember a couple of times when the soldiers passed through, and then they only wanted the chickens that were feeding in the front yard. Once a soldier picked up a long bamboo stick (which we used for drying the laundry when it was not raining), whacked some chickens, and took them away.

The next few years were quite uneventful. I got along with my cousins quite well, except for Pock Face. He usually liked to boss us around. As a result, I tried hard to stay out of his way.

I can not remember if I ever thought about or missed my parents during this time. I rarely got to see my older sister and brother, so I did not have much of an impression of them either. One day, after I had turned eight and the war was about over (I didn't know about, care about, or understand the fighting), Uncle waved a letter in front of me and told me that my parents were coming to pick me up and take me *home* with them. I thought Uncle's house was my home. Uncle showed me a photo which was enclosed with the letter and told me that the couple in the picture were my parents. I thought they were very beautiful. They were dressed in clothing unlike any I had ever seen. I started to fantasize about what life would be like living with my own parents.

Finally, one early summer day in 1945, my parents arrived by boat. My uncle's house was right at the water's edge, and the kitchen partially extended over the water. Our dead-end part of the stream was connected to a river that ran nearby, making transportation by boat quite convenient. Recently, my mother told me that the "house" was a part of a much bigger residence my paternal grandfather had inherited and expanded. After he passed away the house was divided into four parts. Each of my father's brothers occupied a quarter, and ran their own respective households. I never knew which portion of the house belonged to my father, since as far back as I could remember my parents had never stayed in their portion of the house.

I rushed down to the dock as the boat was arriving to meet my parents. Suddenly I could not speak, although I had been practicing in private how to address them as "Ba Ba" and "Ma Ma." It was so unnatural to me to call two total strangers by those names. I guess I eventually came around to addressing them by their proper salutations in the mornings that followed. I only had chance to greet them in the mornings to pay respect and did not have chances to talk to them during the day time since the adults had so much to catch up.

After a few days, it was time for my parents and I to visit Grandfather and pick up my sister and brother. The voyage by boat took a good half-day, and on the way my parents told me that I also had two younger sisters, Shiao Ling and Shiao Yu. I also had a younger brother, but he had been adopted by one of my father's childless friends. At the time he was born, my mother and Shiao Ling were traveling to the war capital, Chongqin, while avoiding the Japanese army. I did not know about this younger brother, Xiao Lung Wang, until several years later. At the time he was not a part of the Chen household.

Chapter II:

The Whole Family United

We spent a few days at Grandfather's house, and I was reacquainted with my sister and brother. I felt so fortunate to be back with them and they were very friendly to me, which was quite a change from the first time we were together. To this day all six of us siblings have been very close emotionally, even though we don't live in the same state or continent physically and only see each other occasionally.

On the day we were leaving for my parents' house in Shanghai, we got up before daybreak, even though the distance from Grandfather's village to Shanghai was less then 120 kilometers. First we had to travel by rowboat to a small town to catch the train. It took more than half a day for the rowboat to reach the town, Xiashi, where I had received the penicillin shot that saved my life. Then we took the train another few hours to get to Shanghai. By the time we got to Shanghai, the street lights were already on. My father, being a colonel in the Shanghai police department, had a car with a driver who came to pick us up. That was the first time I had ever seen an automobile, a small house on wheels. As we rode along the streets of Shanghai, my brother pointed out how big the "candles" (electrical lights on top of a concrete column) were.

My father's house, situated on Avennie Road, (I doubt if that road name still exists) was assigned to him by the Shanghai PD and had three stories with many bedrooms. It was huge! It had a double-wide iron gate to allow the car to pull in. Downstairs, there was the living room, dining room, kitchen and three small bedrooms in the back of the kitchen for the male and female servants and the driver. There were several bedrooms on the second floor and a very large undivided third floor (as I recall). We used the third floor as our study and activity room. The house had high walls and an enclosed large backyard with trees and flowers. It was beautiful. We stayed in that house for less than a year, but it definitely made an impression on me.

About a week or so after we arrived in Shanghai, the vacation was over. My mother hired a tutor for us three older siblings because school would start some time in August. We would be placed in an elementary school nearby. Because of my father's position and connections, we did not have to take the typical entrance examinations. I would start in the third grade while my elder sister and brother would both be in the fifth grade, and Shiao Ling would be in the second grade. I never thought about why Shiao Ling, two years younger than I, would start only one grade below me. The answer came only recently when I asked her about it. She told me that when she was four, Mother enrolled her in kindergarten, a year ahead of most of the kids. That, combined with the fact that her birthday was in January, made her smarter and more mature than kids born in the later part of year. A year later, when Mother started Shiao Ling in the first grade she instructed the young girl to answer, in case any teacher or someone from the school asked about her age, to answer "six." However, Mother did not prepare her for possible follow-up questions. When people at school asked Shiao Ling how old she was last year she answered "four." The teachers let it pass and thought she might be a little confused.

The difficulty of the school's curriculum came as quite a shock. There were mathematics and beginning English in the third grade for me and I did not know how my sister and brother survived being in an ever higher grade. The tutor certainly helped. He came every afternoon when the school was out. After we had our snack we went right to work.

In those days, corporal punishment in class was commonplace. With class sizes usually above sixty students, this was the only way to keep order. After each quiz the ones that scored at the bottom, especially those that scored below sixty out of 100, would have their palms hit by the teacher using a foot-long wooden ruler. The teachers, be they male or female, did not show any mercy. I believe I got hit only once, and as the semester progressed, my grades began to move toward the middle among my fellow students. If I remember correctly I could never score above the eighty-point level.

Sometime during the middle of fall semester, one of us picked up the measles from school and passed it around to all the siblings except Xiao (there was spelling change after the Communists took over the mainland from 'Shiao') Yu. Mother moved a couple of twin beds into the big room on the third floor and made it into a hospital ward for all four sick kids. We all missed about a week of school because of the measles.

Toward the end of the semester, my father changed jobs. First he was assigned to work for the Zhejiang provincial government in Hangzhou (the provincial capitol). Since Zhejiang government did not have a residence ready for our family, Father went ahead and bought a small house for thirty taels of gold (about forty ounces) and waited until the school year was over to move us. In the meantime my father's job assignment changed again. This time he was to go with the governor of Zhejiang, Chen Yi, to Taiwan (commonly known as Formosa at the time) to establish a provisional government after Taiwan reverted back to China (in 1945) after fifty years of Japanese occupation.

Since there was a fully furnished house for the family in Taipei, Taiwan near the provisional office building (later on it became the presidential office building), Father decided most of us would spend the winter school vacation with him and continue the spring semester at a grade school in Taipei. Again according to Mother, Shiao Hui and Hsiao Tsung did not join the rest of the family in Taipei because they had more school work to catch up on. They stayed with a friend of our parents during the winter vacation and boarded at the school when classes were in session. Mother took the three of us, Shiao Ling, Xiao Yu, and I, to Taiwan by ship.

We enjoyed Taiwan very much because the climate was mild. There was no snow in winter, and we were able to get watermelon in the cold months, a real treat.

Little did we know that although Taiwan now belonged to China, most of the residents age fifty and under only remembered the Japanese occupation. They did not think that they were ethnic Chinese originally from the mainland. They resented the newly arrived mainlanders and the new rules that came with them. On February 28, 1946, (the famous 2/28 incident), there was a revolt by some of the islanders. They attacked some of the government offices, minor military depots, and any of the mainlanders who happened to be on the streets.

Throughout the night there was machine-gun fire from a military installation (the fort is still there to this day) near the front door of our house. The house was walled, with a large, beautiful back yard, and faced a six-lane-wide street (the residence is now rebuilt and houses the department of education). We all huddled in the stairwell and did not dare to go upstairs to our bedrooms. When morning came, the gun was silent. We went upstairs and saw a bullet hole in one window. The bullet had traveled the length of the hallway and embedded in the wall opposite the window. While we were looking out the window onto the street, we saw a man armed with a long Japanese samurai sword on his back loitering at our front door. It was a good thing Father had had the foresight of putting a local-sounding name (Chen Shao Huo instead of his real name, Chen Shao Ying) on the front door. After a while the man left, satisfied that the residents must be Taiwanese.

In late March of that year, Father decided it was too dangerous for Mother and us young ones to remain in Taiwan due to events and the possibility of another revolt. We were pulled out of school after a little more than a month and went back to the mainland.

I remembered very little about the school I went to in Taipei, but I do remember that there was a morning break around 10 AM. The school served free warm milk to all the students. All we needed to do was to bring our own tin cup and sugar for the milk. I believe it was powdered milk from U.S. war surplus.

Since we already owned a house in Hangzhou we went directly there upon returning to the mainland. Again Mother had to make arrangements for me (still in third grade) and Shiao Ling (second grade), to be enrolled in our respective grades in the middle of the spring semester. Since my older sister and brother had only one year to go before graduating from the grade school (sixth grade), they continued at the boarding school in Shanghai.

I do not remember the name of the grade school I first entered during the second half of the spring semester of the third grade. During the fourth grade, Mother switched me to another school. I believe it was the grade school attached to the Hong Dao Girls High School. Again, I did not know any of the kids in my class. The only person I remember was this big girl who sat in the back of the class. She had light hair and did not look at all Chinese. Later on I found out that she was the granddaughter of President Chiang Kai Shek. Her mother was from Russia. During the fifth grade, I had the fortune to have President Chiang's eldest grandson in my class. He was a few years older than most of the kids. At the beginning of the sixth grade (1948), Mother switched me again to a grade school that was very close to our home, and I graduated from that school. The name of the school was Yeou Sun Quan Yang Elementary School. Many years later, during the summer of 1984, when I accepted a visiting professorship at the Zhejiang National University in Hangzhou, my brother, Xiao Lung, took me to visit the school. I had no memory of the old school after thirty-five years.

During all the time we were moving around, we did not see our father at all. It was Mother who made all the decisions of switching schools for Shiao Ling and I. Mother was a graduate of a teacher's normal school (the equivalent of regular three-year high school but with an emphasis on teaching methods). It was rare before 1918 that girls went to any school beyond grade school. Our mother also taught a few years of kindergarten after she graduated. From 1941to 1944 (I believe), when she was in the war capital, Chongqin, with the encouragement of Father and his boss she established Woo Dei Elementary School and was its inaugural principal.

Despite the frequent interruptions of our schooling caused by moves, my mother often thought ahead when it came to our academics. Once we caught up with the curriculum presented to us in the school we jumped into mid-semester, it was time to switch to a more challenging school. Her strategy was validated when we had no trouble getting into top schools or colleges (by way of entrance exams) after we later returned to Taiwan.

CHAPTER III:

Life Under the Communist Government

After Japan's unconditional surrender to China ended the war, we thought life would be calm and we would live happily ever after as a normal family. But the leader of the Chinese Communist party, Chairman Mao Tse Tung, had other ideas. He was busily preparing his army, with the direct help of Union of Soviet Socialist Republic leader Joseph Stalin, to take over all of China. President Chiang Kai Shek saw Mao's ambitions, and tried to stop the Communist (Red) army. His effort was hindered on two fronts. First, China had been at war for decades, and people were leery of another war. Second, the United States did not want to see China experience a civil war. In 1947, U.S. President Harry Truman sent Secretary of State George Marshall to convince Chiang to back off. Marshall paid a total of seven visits to Chiang, and ultimately threatened that the United States would withhold all military support, including but not limited to funds, weapons, and munitions. Finally Chiang had to agree. He still hoped that the Communists would be satisfied to occupy, with help from Stalin, the territories north of the Yangtze River.

But that is enough postwar history and rehashing of the one-sided Chinese civil war; one can always go to history books for more details.

We did have more than a year of calm prior to the Communists crossing the Yangtze River. During the summer of 1947, since we did not have too much studies to catch up on, Mother sent us to spend over a month at our grandfather's house. We sat under the canopy

11

of live grapevines and some times even sampled the sour grapes. We swam in the river in front of his house and caught smelt using round, large, flat bamboo trays that were used in raising silkworms during late fall. We never had such a good time.

In late 1947 or early 1948, Father's job changed again. He was assigned by the provincial governor to be the Chief Administrator of a county, Jia Shan Xian, in Zhejiang Province. Because of our ongoing schooling, we stayed put in Hangzhou, but we got to visit Father and spent the New Year (during our schools' winter recesses) at his official residence, a big house with a big yard. The residence had uniformed guards stationed on both sides of the front entrance. They would salute us when we entering or leaving the residence.

Father had a personal rickshaw to transport him between his office and residence. His official bodyguard would run along side of the rickshaw with his sidearm drawn, finger on the trigger. Father told the guard to put away the gun after the first few days because he might hurt some bystanders in case he tripped and the gun went off. Father had some great plans for the residents of the county: building schools, a hospital, and paving some roads, etc. Some of the proposed projects barely had been approved by the provincial government before the Communist army was on its way.

Early in 1948, Father received orders to shut down the Jia Shan Xian government, and dispose of the Xian's (County's) official seal (a seal about three inches square for issuing official documents) and weapons, so they wouldn't fall into the hands of Communist militias or local hoodlums. In fact, the Communists recruited some of the local hoodlums to be their eyes and ears in tracking government officials in the area. Those people would know who had money and influence locally before the Communists came.

After the Xian government shut down, Father was officially out of a job. He came home to Hangzhou after he closed down the Xian office. The Communist army had already occupied Hangzhou, so he stayed at home for only one night. The Communists had sent out people to look for him. They wanted to arrest and try Father because he was a member of the Kuomintang Party and had been working for the Kuomintang government all his working life, with the exception of when he was a Chinese herb doctor in his early twenties. The sentence at the Communists' so-called "public trials" was always death. The Communist army did not disturb us at the beginning, but later on when they needed something they would come to ask to "borrow" it. We would never see the item again. One time on my way to school I saw a big gathering with two people tied up on a stage. The crowd was shouting at them, and some threw rocks at them. I quickly went away and never found out what ever happened to those two people. I believe that was one such "public trial."

Father's cautious moves were well justified. A few days after he left Hangzhou some people came knocking on our door looking for him. We did not know where he had gone, although we had some inkling that he must have gone to Shanghai because it was a big city and he still had many friends there. They questioned Mother as to his whereabouts for a long time but she did not tell them anything so they left. We believed Mother knew where Father stayed in Shanghai but she did not tell any of us just in case those people came back and started questioning us. Later in the spring, it took Mother many telephone calls to all the friends she knew in Shanghai before she finally located Father. Shortly after that she left us to go to Shanghai to be with him for a short while. Father had to keep moving. Shanghai was not a safe place for him either.

Some time in the summer, Father got his next assignment, working for the provincial government in Taiwan. One evening, Father boarded a motorized sailboat (or Chinese junk) from Shanghai for an offshore island called Zhou Shan. Although the island was only about 30 kilometers from the mainland, it is over 120 kilometers from Shanghai. It took the boat, not quite seaworthy, several days to get there. The junk did not have many amenities, such as a bathroom for example. When Father had to go, he had to visit the stern, tightly hold the rail, and do his business. He told us that he was seasick the whole trip.

Since Father did not know anybody on Zhou Shan Island, he spent the next few months at a temple. The monks treated him well until he was able to arrange a passage to Taiwan, some 700 kilometers away. Mother came home after Father left Shanghai. She lost all contact with him until he reached Taiwan.

That trip took Father more than three weeks. Again, he was seasick most of the way. Father arrived in Taiwan in late fall. He immediately got in touch with Mother by mail via a friend in Hong Kong. It took the letter about a month to get to Hangzhou from Taipei, because the friend in Hong Kong had to shred the Taiwan envelope and put the letter in a new one mailed from Hong Kong. Father wrote in code, so Mother had to explain to us what he meant. Father wanted Mother to arrange for herself (excluding the kids), the uncle I lived with between age six and eight, and Father's cousin to travel to Taiwan as soon as possible, before the Communists tightened the borders.

Before she left, she told us, mostly to Xiao Hui (fourteen years old) and Hsiao Tsung (thirteen) what to do. She told us younger children to listen to the older ones because from then on, they would be in charge of the household. If people inquired about the whereabouts of our mother, we were to say she left for Shanghai because Father was seriously ill. After a month, we would pretend that Mother had sent word that Father had passed away. We were to set up a mourning hall in the front hall of the house, furnish it with his framed picture on the wall, an urn to burn incense in, and two candles. We were to place dishes of fruit or pastries in the mourning room every day for the first couple of months. A month or so after Father's fake demise, we were to tell people that Mother had taken ill and could not come back. If necessary we were to also pretend Mother had died, because we knew she was supposed to be on her way to Taiwan directly from Shanghai. This all took place in 1948.

Mother left money for groceries and household expenses. The house was already paid for. She also told the two older children that she had left three equal amounts of gold bullion (each deposit was 10 taels, about 13 ounces) with three of our most faithful and trustworthy friends. When the household money ran out, Xiao Hui was to go to these friends to retrieve the gold and sell it for expenses. According to Mother, in the end Xiao Hui got the full amount from Xiao Lung's adoptive parents, half from another friend, and nothing but tears from the third one. I learned later that Mother arrived in Taiwan in fall 1948. She and two uncles first went to Hong Kong by train and then waited for Father to send the entrance permits to Taiwan. Because the permits only had a thirty-day window of validity, they went to Taiwan from Hong Kong by steamer.

Meanwhile, the five of us were left to our own devices. When Mother left, Xiao Hui and Hsiao Tsung were both in the third year of junior high (ninth grade). Shiao Ling was in her last year of grade school and Xiao Yu was in second grade. In the early summer of 1949, I graduated from grade school, passed the entrance examination, and was enrolled in the Middle School of the Zhejiang University (much later, in the summer of 1984, I was a visiting professor at the same university). Even though our home was twenty minutes away, I boarded at the school as Mother wished. I usually went home Saturday afternoon (because we had classes on Saturday morning) and returned to the dormitory Sunday afternoon before supper.

Since the government paid for most of the cost of running the school, the students paid very little, even for boarding students. As a result, the quality of the food was very poor. During the fall of 1949 (my first semester at the school), the food was so bad that some of us started talking about a dog that was always in and out of the school kitchen. We talked to a cook in the kitchen about the possibility of eating the dog. He said if we killed it, he would skin and cook it. We made some preparations (namely, found a club and stole some telephone wire). During a weekend when there were very few students staying at school, we put the plan into action. I went into the kitchen with the club in hand and chased the dog toward the door where two fellow students with the wire loop were waiting. We clubbed the dog when its head was caught in the loop until it fell. After that I went home for the weekend. When I came back the next day for supper, my friends had saved me a piece of the dog meat, cooked in soy sauce; that was really delicious. We talked about doing it again in the future with another dog but no other dogs had ever appeared in the kitchen area or around the school. It could be that the other dogs got smart or they were all eaten.

In the fall of 1950, there was an older student who moved into our dorm room (which housed twelve to sixteen students at any given time). He was about three years older than most of us. He was very friendly toward two of the kids. At first I did not pay much attention to what were going on, but I started to notice that he got into bed with one of them from time to time. One night he came to my bed and started to touch me and sexually abuse me. He wanted me to reciprocate. I started to cough violently and he was afraid I might throw up on him so he moved away. He repeated his visit a couple more times before I left school and started the journey to Taiwan. As an adult, whenever I read or hear about boarding schools, these images pop into my mind.

During the same semester, the school wanted us to make soy milk that could be sold. We had to get up around 5 AM. The cooks presoaked the soy beans the night before so we could grind them into a paste and use cloth bags to squeeze the soy milk out. The cooks boiled the milk in a big kettle and bottled it for the older kids, who used bicycles to deliver the bottles to customers. The school kept most of the profits but the cooks occasionally got some of the proceeds. When that happened we might have some meat for supper. I was so proud of my contribution to the effort that I even wrote about it in a letter to my parents.

In the fall of 1949, Grandpa came to live with us in Hangzhou. He left the big house he had spent a lifetime building. The year before, when the Communist army first came to his village, they arrested him for no reason, other than that he was a landowner. He leased his land to farmers and collected a portion of the crops as rent payment. The Communists accused him of oppressing the farmers, even though his tenants all felt he was very fair and generous. They demanded that he pay a fine of 25 dans (100 Chinese catties, or 50 kilograms, per dan) of rice before he would be released. Grandfather gave all he had and Mother made up the shortage. Later, some farmer in the village sent him a message that the Communists planned to arrest him again and this time they wanted 75 dans of rice. Mother asked Grandfather to come to Hangzhou to live with us before their next extortion attempt, because the price of rice had risen greatly due to the war. Mother would not be able to cover the cost of rice for him next time. So at the urging of the farmer friend, he left immediately.

When Grandfather reached Hangzhou, Mother had already left town for Shanghai. He was very depressed. He hoped some day the Kuomintang's army would defeat the Communists and he could return home. It was never meant to be.

One summer day, he and I walked to a farmer's market to buy eggs, because produce was cheaper there. It took us about an hour to get there and we bought a basket full of eggs. We were pretty happy because indeed it was cheaper. On the way home, it started to rain and soon it was pouring. I convinced Grandfather to hire a rickshaw so we wouldn't be soaked. It took him a while to agree to the idea. The rickshaw was small and narrow. I had to sit on his lap with the basket of eggs at our feet. It took the rickshaw driver less than half an hour to deliver us home, but Grandpa was not happy, because the cost of the rickshaw far exceeded the savings on the eggs.

By the time we got home, one of his legs was numb and he could hardly walk. He came down with fever and went directly to bed. He could not get out of bed for several days. Through a family friend, Xiao Hui got a Chinese herb doctor to pay him a visit. The diagnosis was that he had a mild stroke. He was about seventy-three years old. From then on, we took turns attending to him whenever he needed to use the restroom, bathe, get out of bed, get dressed, eat, etc.

In October of 1950, we got word through Father's friend in Hong Kong that we ought to get ready to travel to Taiwan. Father had a local friend, Mr. Chiang, Xue-bai, who would accompany us to Hong Kong. We had a family meeting, the four of us, as to who would go and who would stay. The conclusion was that since Grandfather could not travel, Xiao Hui would stay to take care of him. Xiao Yu was too young (seven years old). Mr. Chiang didn't quite like the idea of travelling with a small child. So it was decided only the three of middle siblings, Hsiao Tsung, Shiao Ling, and I, would be taking the trip.

Chapter IV:

Journey to Taiwan

The trip was planned for us by Mr. Chiang. First we would take the train from Hangzhou to a small town, I don't remember its name, south of Kwangzhou, capital of Kwangtung province. Mr. Chiang, who was fluent in Cantonese, would locate a local smuggler to take us over the water to Macau for about $300 American, although Hsiao Tsung disputed the sum. Mr. Chiang would then find some way to smuggle us from Macau to Hong Kong, since we did not have entrance permits to Hong Kong.

So the trip began. First we needed to obtain a traveling permit from the local Communist government in order to buy train tickets. Xiao Hui and Hsiao Tsung went to the local government office. They were able to convince the local official that the three of us needed to go to Shanghai to visit our mother because she had taken ill after Father "passed away." The official asked if the rest of the family were going. My siblings told him that Grandfather had had a stroke and could not travel and Xiao Yu was too young. The official was satisfied and issued the travel permit for the three of us without even spelling out where we were going. That permit allowed us to buy train tickets to Kwantung province.

The next few days we spent buying and packing our luggage. Xiao Hui and Hsiao Tsung went to visit Father's friends about getting some of the gold back for the trip and expenses. We also hid a piece of gold (about one tael) inside a deflated leather soccer ball. We attached the gold using medical adhesive tape deep inside the ball then stuffed the ball deep down into a duffle bag. The gold survived the trip to Taiwan and Mother was pleased. We also packed some of our parents' winter overcoats. Some were made of fur. We obviously did not travel light. We each had a couple pieces of luggage.

We decided not to tell anybody about or notify our schools about our pending travel, because that could raise suspicions and foil our plan. In those days one did not know whom to trust.

One evening in November 1950, we boarded the train toward Kwantung province. There were some armed soldiers around the train station and they asked some routine questions. After we showed them our traveling permit and train tickets, they waved us on. To save money we bought the cheapest tickets. Our train stopped at almost every little station along the way. Our 1,100 kilometer (688 miles) journey took about thirty hours. The next morning, the train stopped at Nanchang, the capitol of Kiangsi province. We were all hungry, since there was no food sold on the train. We bought a small basket of tiny oranges and other things from peddlers on the train platform. I must have overindulged on the oranges because a few hours later I had the worst urge to go. There was only one bathroom at the end of each car; I ran through several cars but the bathrooms were all occupied. By the time I finally found one available I had already soiled my underpants. My only option was to take the underpants off, use them to clean myself, and throw them down the toilet onto the railroad tracks. I did not have any underpants on until we got into our hotel room in Macau.

By the time we got to our destination, it was almost the middle of the night on the second day. Mr. Chiang was able to book a small motorized junk to take us to Macau. Actually, traveling during the night had its advantages, namely the armed guards on the Chinese side were sleeping so they did not take any shots at us. It took all night to reach Macau, a distance of about 60 kilometers. I believe the reason we were smuggled to Macau was because it was not guarded. That situation changed shortly.

After we checked into a hotel, Mr. Chiang managed to make contact with Father's friend, a Mr. Ho (an accountant, according to

Hsiao Tsung) in Hong Kong about the remainder of our trip and found out that our entrance permits to Taiwan had expired. We were short on funds so Mr. Ho needed to contact Father to inform him about our arrival in Macau and need for money. We holed up in the hotel for the next two weeks or so waiting for the money. Mr. Chiang was mostly gone during the days and he only came back to take us to restaurants for supper. We later found out that he spent most of his days in the casino. He also pawned the more valuable items, such as the fur coats, to support his gambling. In a way this was good for us, because it reduced the size of our luggage. Besides there was no need for heavy coats in Taiwan.

Soon Mr. Chiang found out that there was no way Father could get him an entrance permit to Taiwan, since he was not a direct relative and he had never worked in the government. Ten days or so after we got to Macau he went home. He left us to fend for ourselves with next to nothing, except the luggage. Hsiao Tsung was now in charge. We would buy a box of pastries to eat sparingly during the day and at supper time we went to a small restaurant and shared a small pot of steamed rice with a Chinese sausage on top of it. We usually ordered additional rice. Fortunately the soy sauce was free. The one decent thing Mr. Chiang did was informing Mr. Ho in Hong Kong about his departure. A few days later Mr. Ho, through a friend in Macau, managed to send enough money to pay the hotel bill. Mr. Ho also arranged for us to be smuggled into Hong Kong.

On the day of our voyage to Hong Kong, we were escorted to the cabin of the ferry boat's first mate (I do not remember his name). The trip only took about five hours. After the ship arrived in Hong Kong and all the passengers had disembarked, we remained on board until after dark. Leaving the ferry, we carried the remaining luggage between the three of us and walked toward the exit gate on the pier. There was a lone armed guard at the gate. We were so worried about how we were to pass the guard, but we kept on walking. Just when we were about to reach the gate the guard conveniently turned his back (obviously this was also prearranged and paid for). We walked right behind him, out the opened gate and onto the streets of Hong

Kong. We had no idea how much it cost Father to have Mr. Ho arranged all this.

Just a few steps later, Mr. Ho and his daughter, in her late teens, came over and introduced themselves. They took us on a bus to a small hotel. We were given some Hong Kong dollars and Mr. Ho told us that we needed to stay there for a few days until the Taiwan entrance permits arrived. That few days turned out to be another two weeks. Once we got the permits Mr. Ho booked passage on a ship for Taiwan. In the meantime the girl, Miss Ho, came by every few days and took us sightseeing in Hong Kong and treated us to meals at fancy restaurants. Otherwise we just ate at a small neighborhood restaurant. On one outing she even took some pictures for us (the first pictures of me in my whole life). Mr. Ho explained the reason that we could not stay with his family was because housing was very expensive and he only had a small apartment. We were invited to his home for a meal once and saw that he only had a two-room walkup for a family of four. I believe he also had a younger son.

Figure 1: Shiao Hsiung, Hsiao Tsung and Shiao Ling looking down from Kowloon across to Hong Kong circa December 25, 1950.

A couple days before a new year began, we were finally on our last leg of the journey to Taiwan. We were very excited. We had no problems getting on the ship. The Hong Kong government did not care about people leaving, as it only restricted the people entering. To save money, we were booked in third-class berths (the cheapest passage). We were in a hold below the main deck filled with perhaps a hundred narrow bunk beds. I will never forget the stench of the hold, a mixture of vomit and diesel fuel (I only realized later that it was diesel fuel I was smelling). Our bags were placed next to our beds since there was no other place to store them. It took two days and two nights to cross the 840 kilometers (525 miles) of the Taiwan Strait, a notoriously rough sea. We were so seasick that we did not even bother to find out where and when meals were served on board. At one point I became very thirsty. I managed to find a station on the main deck that had a tank that held tea, cold of course. I filled my stomach with it and felt good until I walked by an open door, looked out at the sea, and threw it all up. As the tea was passing through my throat on the way out it was still cold. Otherwise, we stayed in our bunks most of the time and vomited on the floor just like everyone else did.

We arrived in Keelung, Taiwan in the morning of New Years Day, 1951. Disembarkation was uneventful. We had no personal identification except the entrance permits. At customs, we had nothing to declare except our luggage. We saw Father for the first time over almost two years. I cannot remember my emotions at the time, except that I thought he was much shorter than I remembered.

Since Father was working for the Taiwan provincial government, he had a house assigned and partially furnished by the government. It was a reasonably large and comfortable house. Neighbors were mostly his colleagues. For transportation, the government furnished him with a pedicab and a driver, Mr. Lee. The pedicab was wider than a rickshaw and had room to seat two adults (Chinese size) comfortably or three kids. We usually did not ask Mr. Lee to take us on non-official business trips when Father was not using the cab. Mr. Lee worked for Father for several years until he retired and started his own bicycle repair shop.

CHAPTER V:

Junior High School and College

After a few days rest, Mother got us a tutor to start our studies again. We missed the last third of the fall semester during our travels, and school would be starting again in February after the winter break. We did not want to sit out another semester. To avoid repeating the same grade, we really hit the books hard. We could not enroll in decent schools in Taipei without passing entrance examinations. Mother had a friend who was able to convince the principal in a secondary school outside Taipei City to let us enroll for the spring semester after some simple tests. Since we came from Hangzhou, we did not have any documents to verify that we were ever in any schools. All three of us entered the Ban Qiao High School (almost all the so-called high schools have three years of junior high and three years of high school). Hsiao Tsung would continue his first year in high school, I would be in the second year of junior high (equivalent to eighth grade), and Shiao Ling would be in her first year of junior high.

The town of Ban Qiao is located outside the city of Taipei. Every school day we had to go from our home to the Taipei train station (it would take about twenty minutes on a bicycle), take the train (about half an hour) to Ban Qiao, and walk the rest of the way to school. There was no public transportation to take us from home to the train station so we quickly learned to ride a bicycle. Shiao Ling was a little shaky on the bike at the beginning, so I volunteered to carry her on my bike at the beginning of the semester until a couple of weeks later we had a spill and both of our knees were skinned. She decided to learn to ride. The classes were not so difficult even though we missed part of the fall semester. By the end of spring semester, I was placed in the top quarter of the class and Shiao Ling did even better. In order to avoid the daily commute to Ban Qiao when the fall semester started again, we all decided to take the entrance examinations for the top high schools in Taipei. Needless to say, our tutoring continued through the summer recess.

At the beginning of the fall semester 1951 we all took our respective exams. Luckily both I and Shiao Ling were admitted to the junior high school at the National Normal University, but Hsiao Tsung missed by a small margin. Since there were only a few spaces in each class, the acceptance rate was less than 10 percent. Hsiao Tsung decided to stay at Ban Qiao High School. He graduated at near the top of his class. Later on he successfully passed the entrance examination to study at the Tainan College of Engineering (now the National Cheng Kong University), majoring in chemical engineering.

The class I was admitted to for my last year of junior high was identified as junior high class Number 26. There were four classes at the same grade, namely, Numbers 25, 26, 27, and 28, each consisting of about sixty students. The last year of junior high soon came to an end and we graduated in early June, 1952 before the end of the normal semester. We even had to take a graduation examination on top of the normal final exam. I never understood the significance of that examination.

On the day of graduation, there was an incident that I believe is worthy of mention. There was a boy in class 28. I was told students in that class had the lowest scholastic achievements because many of the students were orphans who had lost one or both parents in the Sino-Japanese War. They had a tougher life. This boy graduated with all of us. On my way home he caught up with me and forced me off my bike. He was very athletic with big muscles. He said he intended to beat me up for frequently looking at him at school. He asked me if I would submit willingly. I told him I would like to have a chance to explain why I looked at him so often. Certainly he could have easily beat me up. The reason I watched him at school was because I admired him, his athletic abilities, on the parallel bars and chin-up bars, and the fact that he was on the boxing team, which I could never be. I meant no disrespect to him at all. He was obviously satisfied with my explanation, so he let me go without laying a finger on me. Actually he was not the first bully I had encountered. There was one case where I ran into a guy on the train on the way to Ban Qiao. I did not know what I had done to offend him but he pushed me around a bit. For a while I just tried to avoid him and not to be in the same car with him.

Soon after graduation, it was entrance examination time again. I had the option to take the test for high school at the same school or two other top high schools in Taipei, or to take the examination to the Taipei Institute of Technology (TIT), bypassing the three-year senior high for a five-year technical education. My parents left it entirely up to me. So as not to take any chances, I took both tests(fortunately they were not scheduled on the same days). The final results were favorable to me. I successfully passed both entrance examinations. The admittance rates were both about 20 percent. Since I did not enjoy the subjects of history (some five-thousand-plus years of Chinese history) and geography (China is a large country, plus the rest of the world) I opted to go to TIT, majoring in mechanical engineering. There were forty students admitted into that class out of 250-plus students that took the examinatio. I had already chosen my career path at the age of fifteen. It turned out I still had to take a semester of modern Chinese history (which I barely passed), but no geography classes.

The curriculum for the five years at TIT was a mixture of high school and college level classes. We had three years each of English and Chinese. We had trigonometry, geometry and college algebra. Calculus and differential equations were a total of three semesters, all taught by the same teacher. He did a good job in teaching calculus and spent two and a half semesters on the subject, but only barely touched on differential equations. We were fortunate to have many of the college-level classes taught by professors who also taught the same subjects at National Taiwan University.

We had one teacher who taught us thermodynamics. He was very conscientious in his work. We normally had three-hours of scheduled class a week, but he would frequently conduct extra classes for two more hours on Saturday afternoons. His tests were usually killers. I remember that at the end of the semester, only I and two other classmates out a total of forty passed the final exam. Everyone complained bitterly behind his back. He was one of three teachers who stand out in my memory, the other two being the English teacher, Mr. Yang, and the calculus teacher. Unfortunately I cannot remember all their names. During the entire five years, I deeply appreciated their dedication.

These five years were the most peaceful and uneventful period of my life. I spent all five years in one school, one class, no moving around. TIT was located only about twenty minutes by bicycle from my home (the one we moved into in 1952). By that time, Father already had two job changes. First he was named by the provincial government to be the chief of the taxation bureau of Taipei. He resigned after a year. The reasons were that the job was too busy and the pay was low. During festival times many people all wanted to give him gifts, and invariably almost all the gift packages had cash stuffed in them. He had straight orders to never accept any "gifts". He was afraid that even if he refused all the gifts, someone might still accuse him of taking bribes. He wanted to get out of that job before anything bad happened. Later on he was assigned to serve as the inspector general of the First Commerce Bank of Taiwan, in which the provincial government had roughly 60 percent ownership. We moved to a bank-owned house on Ning Po East Street. This house had both front and back yards, fruit trees, and a small fish pond. The home had three bedrooms plus servant quarters. Father stayed at this job until he retired. The pay was the same grade as the general manager of the bank. He was not so busy and was respected by the top executives of the bank. In addition to this job, he was also a member of the National Assembly. He had been a member since about 1950.

There had been a nationwide election in 1947, the first and only general election in the Republic of China to choose members of the National Assembly, one from each xian of each province. More than 3,300 delegates were elected. The members of National Assembly would elect the president and vice-president and amended the constitution if needed. Father ran in that first election , bidding for the seat for Hai Yen Xian (his birth place) in Zhejiang province. He was narrowly defeated. After the Nationalist government fled the mainland, many of the elected members were either killed by the Communists or never made it to Taiwan. The person who beat out Father in the election did not make to Taiwan. Per the constitution's rules regarding substitution, Father was named the official representative of Hai Yen Xian for the 1950 National Assembly meeting.

Chapter VI:

Met My Sweetheart and Lifetime Companion

During the summers of 1955 and 1956, I participated in a government-sponsored summer camp where I learned to drive. Each camp was four weeks long. There were about 400 students total in the camps for both years. Participants were college or high school students (with a minimum age of seventeen). They were all honor students recommended by their respective schools. Competition for a place in the summer camps was very keen, because the government provided the entire cost for the camp (including room and board) and very few students could find summer jobs in Taiwan. I participated the second time in 1956 as a member of the advanced platoon, a total of twenty members out of the previous years' several hundred. There also was an platoon of twenty-six female students. During roll call, the female platoon was out in front of the formation and our advanced platoon lined up right behind them. That gave us "second timers" a great opportunity to check them out.

Out of the twenty-six girls, I noticed a pretty one in the middle of the second row, lined up just in front of me. She was thin with big eyes. She had very pale skin, looking almost sickly. She was usually very quiet. Many times I stood there imagining what a date with her would be like, what we would do, what we would talk about. I had never dated a girl before in my nineteen years. How could I approach her to ask for a date? Not even knowing her name made it more difficult. I would not and could not ask any fellow campers for advice, because I did not want anyone to know that I was interested in her.

The male students drove two-and-a-half-ton GMC trucks and the female students drove weapon carriers, the forerunner of modern-day Hummers (I believe). We had classes in addition to the actual driving training. Half the classes were civics and "Three People's Principles," and the rest were on the mechanics of the automobile. I was picked by the camp director to be the lecturer on the subject of internal combustion engines. This was likely because I had just studied the subject matter during the previous semester at TIT and was an advanced camper. The director was short of instructors in this subject area. Of course, it was a big honor for me to get up on the big stage and lecture to a class of 400.

On the morning of the lecture, I was very nervous about my lesson. Besides, there she was, sitting right in the center of the front row. She was right in front of me and looked up at me with her lovely big eyes, pencil in hand, ready to take notes. I had prepared the lecture and conferred with the camp director about how deep into the subject I should go. I wrote out my lecture notes and prepared some simple illustrations. But when the time came and I opened my mouth, no sound came out. If there had been a hole on the stage, I would have crawled into it right away. My awkwardness was so funny that the class roared with laughter until the camp director stepped to the front of the stage and quieted them. I managed to get underway. Following my written notes, I did fine, as long as I avoided looking at her.

After that lecture, I became somewhat of a celebrity around the camp. Some of the girls would take the initiative to say hello to me. Some even introduced themselves by telling me their names. So one day I got up enough courage, and waited for the opportunity. When we passed each other and she smiled at me, I asked her name. She told me her name was Shun Chih Weng. We talked a little bit, and she told me she came from a high school with an emphasis on business in Kaohsiung. She had one more year to go before graduating.

The ice was broken, but we still did not have many chances to talk to each other. As a matter of fact, the girls kept to themselves. A female army captain, the girl's platoon officer, made very sure that they did. Boys could only admire them from a distance. The summer campers were divided into eight or nine platoons, each with an army officer, usually a captain, as its "monitor." If a camper had personal business that required leaving camp for a short while, they had to obtain permission from the monitor. Actually, all the summer camps (there were several summer camps in different subject areas, mountain climbing being another focus) were run in a quasi-military style. We all wore army fatigues as our uniform. Our camp director was an old army colonel. Our driving instructors were all career army sergeants. They all carried a screwdriver, and they would hit your leg if there was any grinding of the gears when shifting. I do not know if they hit the girls also. The GMC trucks had five forward gears. One had to double-clutch when shifting, especially when downshifting or shifting into the reverse gear. To shift into the reverse gear, the truck had to be completely stopped or the gears would grind and the gearbox would sound like it was about to explode.

The time went by quickly at summer camp, which was busy but enjoyable. During the last week of the camp I finally gathered enough courage to ask Shun Chih to spend the last Sunday with me (we only got Sundays off for personal time). She agreed. By that time many of her fellow female campers had already been talking about how Shun Chih and I were an "item." She did not argue much with them (as she told me later).

Sunday came and we decided to go the Yuan Shan Zoo (Taipei Municipal Zoo) and spend the day there. We took the city bus. I was going to buy the bus tickets, but Shun Chih presented me with tickets she had already purchased. We had a good time at the zoo. When lunch time came, I bought her a bowl of noodles, although she offered to pay. I was so overwhelmed by her actions and attitude during this first date. I knew I was falling hopelessly in love with her.

I had heard that when a boy took a girl out in those days, she would expect a taxi for transportation instead of a pedicab. Taking the city bus was not even a possibility. When they went to a restaurant, she would order a bunch of expensive dishes (of course she expected him to pay) and then say she was not hungry. In those days, doggie bags were not yet invented.

By afternoon, we had seen enough animals for one day. I asked her if she would like to come home with me to meet my parents. She had no objection. When we got home, Mother was working on the manual sewing machine by the window in the dining room. After the introduction, Shun Chih sat down next to Mother and discussed what Mother was doing so naturally, as if they had known each other for a long time. After dinner we stayed as late as possible before we had to go back to camp.

Soon after the summer camp was over, and she had to go home. I promises that I would come to visit her during the winter recess. In the meantime we would write to each other. Her home was in Pingtung, about forty minutes by train or thirty-five minutes by bus from Kaohsiung. Every day she rode her bicycle to the Pingtung train station (the train fare was cheaper), took the train, and then rode the city bus to her school.

In October I learned that a radio station which broadcast island-wide took requests for a certain song to be played on the station at a designated time. I called and then wrote to the station to ask them to play the "Blue Danube Waltz" by Johann Strauss for a Miss Gon-Yu (I broke up her last name into two Chinese characters) in the city of Pingtung at 10 AM on a Sunday morning and the station agreed. I was so excited. I wrote her to tune her radio at that time to listen to it and I would do the same. She wrote me a few days after that particular Sunday that she had heard the waltz. Fifty years later we cruised on the Danube River.

Figure 2: Shun Chih Weng at summer camp for driving, 1956.

My promise that I would visit her in Pingtung during the winter recess (we both were in our final year of our studies) was always on my mind. I did not want to reveal my desire to my parents because I was afraid they might laugh at me or disapprove. In the meantime I concentrated on my studies and my grades improved drastically. Prior to that time, I had only cared about the knowledge I gained. I let the grades be whatever they were (usually in the mid-seventieth percentile, because I usually did not study hard for the final exams). That year was the first time my cumulative average hit the mid-eightieth percentile, placing me in the top three of the class.

I also discovered that a company in Kaohsiung, the Tong Rong Iron Works, a mechanical-engineering-related industry, was accepting a limited number of trainees. I applied for and was accepted for a four-week stint during the winter vacation. Obviously my improved grades had a lot to do with my acceptance. The position came with a small stipend too. My parents happily approved my plan. My uncle (the one I stayed with between the ages of six and eight) happened to work and live in Kaohsiung, and I could stay at his place. So it was all settled. I headed south to Kaohsiung as soon as the final examinations were done and reported to Tong Rong. I would have four weekends to go to Pingtung and to see Shun Chih.

It turned out the living arrangements did not work out well for me. Uncle's wife had been left behind in China, and he had a girlfriend who often came to spend the night with him. Since he had only a one-room apartment, I slept on the couch with their bed just a few feet away. Also, on weekends, my uncle played mahjongg usually past mid-night. I had to wait until they were finished to go to sleep. So on the second Saturday afternoon (Saturday was a half-day at work), I looked around and found a family near Tong Rong that would rent me a closet-sized (under the stairwell) room, about 4 feet by 8 feet on a weekly basis. I informed my uncle and immediately moved in. I told my uncle that because I could not go to bed by ten on Sundays, I felt sleepy on Mondays. He did not object and told me to eat my suppers at his place with his girlfriend. Occasionally his girlfriend would pack the leftovers for my next day's lunch.

I was very happy to have this arrangement. Now I could come and go as I pleased. On Sunday I went to visit Shun Chih and told her about my new place. She was happy for me too. Shun Chih's family lived across from a banana garden so normally her house was pretty quiet, but not on most Sundays. Her home was located only a short bicycle ride from the Pingtung Air Force Base and the Naval Military Base in Zuoying was only about a twenty-minute train ride away. On Sundays, young air force and naval officers in their crisp Sunday uniforms would come calling for her frequently. She told me she usually did not go out with any of them, except one. This boy's sister was in the same high school class with her so she felt some obligation, especially when his sister came visiting too. But that was not very often. I knew she was trying to assure me that she was my girl. I tried not to show any concern or jealousy.

One Sunday, the third one I believe, we decided to pay Hsiao Tsung a visit in Tainan. He was in his last year of college and he had returned to school early after the winter recess. He was very happy to meet Shun Chih. He took us around the campus and some parts of the city near the campus. He treated us to lunch at a restaurant.

He ordered so many delicious dishes that I had to excuse myself so I could loosen my belt.

Soon the winter break was over and I had to be getting back to Taipei. The last Sunday we spent together we went all over Pingtung on bicycles. I borrowed her sister Mei Lai's bike. After supper, when the time came for me to go back to my room in Kaohsiung, she, with her bike, walked all the way to the train station with me. I did not feel comfortable letting her ride home alone in the dark so I walked her home and then rushed back to the station to catch the last train to Kaohsiung.

I felt fairly certain that we would be together for a very long time. I also felt so fortunate that I had found such a beautiful, pure girl without any of the usual bad habits and pretenses.

Chapter VII:

Military Service

My last semester at TIT came to an end, and I graduated in early June 1957. It was the law that every young man must serve in the military at the age of twenty-one. Although I was only twenty at the time, I couldn't wait for a year to serve. Since I had plans to study abroad, most likely in United States, I did not want to lose a year by working somewhere before my military service duty. I requested through the local selective services to go into the air force right away and was approved. Even through Taipei Institute of Technology did not grant us baccalaureate degrees, we were still classified as college graduates. We were to serve in the Reserve Officers Training Corps (ROTC). Each ROTC cadet must serve a total of three years. Our first tour of duty was for eighteen months and then we were temporarily discharged as a reserve officer with the rank of second lieutenant. The second tour of duty, another eighteen months, could come any time after three years.

I did not join the air force to become a pilot. To become a pilot, one must be a graduate of the Air Force Academy. Instead I would serve in one of the support groups as an aircraft maintenance officer. Some of my classmates who went into the army were later stationed in Quemoy and saw some action in 1958 during the August 13 battles with the mainland Chinese.

We all had three months of boot camp, regardless of which branch of service we were in. Then came about four months of technical training to become an air force maintenance officer. Upon finishing we would then be dispatched to various bases around the island to work on military aircraft such as the F-86 (a fighter) or the RF-84 (a reconnaissance plane). These were post-Korean War planes that came from the United States, intended for the protection of Taiwan against any mainland attacks. Because we were college graduates with better-than-average English proficiency, our jobs were to translate the technical manuals from English into Chinese for the technicians to follow.

Another reason I wanted to go into the air Force was because the training camp was located in Donggang, a small fishing town located about thirty-two kilometers southwest of Pingtung. It only took fifty minutes to get to Donggang by train. Although for the first two weeks we were not allowed to leave the base or have any visitors, I knew that would change.

After two weeks we were allowed to have visitors but still confined to the base. Shun Chih came early on the third Sunday to visit me. I kept my cap on the whole time she was there because on the day we reported to camp (arriving around 9 PM from Taipei by train) every recruit had had his head shaved. I did not want her to see my bald head. Only at her insistence did I take the cap off for just a moment. She even brought some delicious dishes for us to share. Beginning on the fifth Sunday we had complete liberty, and since I did not want her to do all the traveling, I went to see her in Pingtung. I was dressed in newly washed and ironed fatigues with no insignia except for a corporal's rank. I ran into some of the young officers from the air force and navy calling on her and I had to salute them, but I did not mind at all because I knew she was with me, a lowly corporal, and I would become a second lieutenant in a few months.

The physical part of the training was hard. We had to crawl on the pitted concrete surface (eroded by the ocean water) under a hot summer sun. For a long time my elbows and knees were all black and blue. But the next seven weeks went by quickly because I always had Sundays to look forward to. We took turns travelling. When she came to visit me we walked around in Donggang. Sometimes we went to the sea side to catch little crabs. I found a small stick and attached a line to it, to fashion a fishing pole. I tied a small piece of chicken (from the mess hall) to the end of the line. When a crab grabbed it, we quickly pulled it out of the water. We threw the crabs back because we did not know what to do with them.

At the end of three months we had a graduation ceremony and we were promoted to sergeants with an increase in pay. Shun Chih came early that day to participate in the occasion.

Figure 3: Second Lieutenant serving in Pingtung, circa 1958.

It was a Saturday morning, and she had to take the half day off work (almost all businesses and governmental offices operated five and a half days per week in Taiwan). She was working in a bank also in Kaohsiung after she graduated from high school. She had to take a test to be accepted to work in the bank.

She sat in the section with relatives and friends of the graduates and proudly watched us stand at attention for the whole event. I also received my assignment to report to the Kangshan air force base for the next part of my training. Kangshan is located about eighteen kilometers north of Kaohsiung and about forty-four kilometers from Pingtung. It would take about an hour from Pingtung by train, with a stop in Kaohsiung, so it was not that far to travel. We were both very happy about my new assignment. I had a few days off before I had to report to my new assignment. I gathered my belongings and went to Pingtung with her, had dinner at her home, and boarded the evening train heading for home in Taipei. Since my train ticket had been supplied by the air force, it was naturally the cheapest kind, and as a result, the train stopped at every little station. The train itself was quite full. Most of those travelling lived in the northern sections of Taiwan, so it was standing room only for most of the trip.

I was among the last few to get on the train before it departed from Pingtung. I barely found a place to stand inside a car. After midnight some of the standing people started to sit down where they had stood. I found that I could not even squat without sitting on someone. By the time the train pulled into Taipei Station (about 10 AM on Sunday), I was so tired I felt like I was walking on clouds.

After a few days of "R & R" at home, I was very anxious to report to my newly assigned base in Kangshan. I would be near Shun Chih again. The first Sunday we were not permitted to leave the base or to have visitors. We were treated much better afterward. There was mostly classroom work with very little boot-camp style physical training.

In the early part of my stay in Kangshan, Shun Chih came on Sundays. We explored Kangshan on foot. On later Sundays we went to Tainan, about twenty-three kilometers north of Kangshan, where we explored many temples, historic sites, and forts. Tainan was one of the oldest urban settlements on the island, made by the Chinese around 1590. The Dutch came in 1623 and stayed until they were driven out around 1661 by Cheng Cheng-Kung, an official of the Qing dynasty. We also walked around the campus of Tainan College of Engineering where Hsiao Tsung obtained his degree. He was also in the service (navy) at the time, stationed in Taipei.

Toward the end of technical training, most of us were getting anxious as to where the next assignment would be. The next assignment would last almost a year, taking us up to discharge. During the second to last week of our technical training, we all talked amongst ourselves about possible bases we would be deployed to. One of the supervising officers, a captain I believe, had been fairly friendly to many of us and leaked some of the information that we were so desperate to know. I found out that my assignment was the air force base right there in Kangshan, a small base. I also happened to find out that my bunkmate was to be assigned to the base in Pingtung. He had just married a few months before, and his home, or rather his parents' home, was in Kangshan. I talked to the captain regarding the criteria for assignments and if the postings were cast in stone. He explained that essentially it was arbitrary, since the higher-ups did not know any of the trainees. Unless some trainee's family knew some colonel or general in the defense department who could send word that so-and-so should be assigned to some particular base, it did not matter where we were sent. Each base had requested a certain number of trained officers based on its needs. The Pingtung air base, a large one, usually made the largest requests. We jokingly called the Pingtung base the bottomless pit. Everyone was afraid of being assigned to it.

So I talked to my bunkmate and asked if he would like to switch assignments with me. If he agreed, I would go and talk to the captain and request that I be allowed to take his place in Pingtung and he would stay in Kangshan. My bunkmate was so grateful he was in tears and almost got down on his knees to thank me profusely. I went to talk to the captain about the switch. He agreed but warned me not to tell anyone, because most of the documents, each individual order (some 300-plus) had already been drawn up. If word got out that swaps were allowed, he would have a mess on his hands. As a matter of fact, he told me to be in his office that evening to rewrite the dispatching orders. I was happy to oblige. As a result, my bunkmate and I knew where we would be going a whole week ahead of most people. I sometimes felt a little guilty because I never told my bunkmate the real reason for the switch, which was not as noble as he thought.

After a few days of rest at home in Taipei I happily reported to Pingtung. I stayed in the bachelors' quarters on base and ate my meals in the mess hall. After about a month or so I, found out it was not that convenient for Shun Chih to visit me. She had to stop at the base gate and register at the guard house before they would then telephone me to come out to accompany her onto the base. First I bought a bicycle so I could go to see her whenever I was off duty. It only took about fifteen minutes from the base to her home and after a while, I found out that I did not need to stay on the base. There was a small restaurant halfway between the base and her home that would accept my air-force-issued meal coupons, so I could eat there. She helped me find a small room in a farmer's family compound. The reason I call it a compound is that he had two rooms next to each other attached to the main house but with separate doors that could be locked individually. It cost $50 New Taiwan dollars a month. The exchange rate those days worked out to about $1.25 American. It was cheap until one considered that my monthly salary as a second lieutenant was only $205 NTD. My rent was a whopping 25 percent of my pay. But I was happy. The room was less than ten minutes' walk from Shun Chih's home. It would only add two more minutes of commuting time to the base by bicycling.

The room was small and had a double-size bed made of bamboo. It made noises if you tossed or turned. The room had a single bare light bulb so it was not dark at night. There was enough room next to the bed to park my bicycle. The room had one window that had sliding wooden slats but no glass. I made a duplicate key to the lock and gave it to Shun Chih. One day while I was at work Shun Chih and her sister, Mei Lai, went in there and put up a curtain they'd made. The wooden slats were not very secure. A tailor-made leather jacket that I hung near the window was stolen one day, obviously through the window slats.

The next room of equal size was rented to a lieutenant in his late twenties from the same base. His name was Fan. Shun Chih and her sister called him "Lao Fan Tongzhi," meaning "old comrade Fan," but they only called him this name behind his back. The two of us usually rode together to work. His reason for not wanting to stay on base was that the bachelors' quarters were too noisy. He needed a quiet place to study for an important examination for a certain grade of civil service after he was discharged from the service. He was a career officer, doing pretty much the same kind of work as I was. I also needed a quiet place to study for the Examination for Studying Abroad, administered by the Ministry of Education. The exam was about a little over a year away, given in the summer. For some reason the department stopped requiring the examination about seven or eight years after I took it. That helped the students who could not pass the exam after multiple tries. Many of my classmates came to the United States to study after that requirement was dropped.

After I moved off the base, we had a lot more time together, Saturday afternoons and Sundays. Occasionally on a Sunday, decked out in my air force blues with my lieutenant's bars on my uniform, I would meet some of the air force and navy guys calling on Shun Chih. They were usually turned away by her sister, who told them that her elder sister was not home, even though Shun Chih was just in the back room. Gradually these guys stopped calling.

Soon I started to hit the books again. My biggest challenge was English. Many people failed to pass the examination because of trouble with English. I only had three years of high-school-level English, and not the additional year of college English most other college graduates had. I had an "Advanced Learner's English Dictionary" which was compiled from English-to-English instead of the typical English-to-Chinese kind. To increase my vocabulary I read the dictionary and all its explanations and examples from time to time. In order to have more study time and yet not neglect Shun Chih, I studied late into the night. Some times I set the alarm clock to wake me up around 1 AM and studied till about 4 in the morning, because I read somewhere that people sleep soundly the first two or three hours and then the two to three hours before they have to get up. The time in between is not as restful. This seemed to work well for me.

When my service came to an end, I had to return to my home in Taipei. During that year, Shun Chih and I had cemented our love for each other. I told her my plans for the future. I wanted (and actually I needed) to study in the United States and get a master's degree, since I did not have a B.S. degree or a high school diploma. I only had my diploma from Taipei Institute of Technology. I would then return to Taiwan and apply for a job with the Tong Rong Iron Works, the place where I had interned during the winter of 1956. To further show my love for her, I saved for a whole year, went to Kaohsiung, and bought her a "nice" watch. It cost two and a half months of my salary at NTD $500. A month before I left Pingtung, I gave it to her. She was very happy to accept and proud to wear it. I did not have the courage to propose to her just yet because I had nothing else to offer her. My future was a big unknown. Unfortunately, I was taken by the watch store. They sold me a lemon. A couple months later, Shun Chih told me that the watch had stopped working and could not be repaired.

Chapter VIII:

Preparation for Studying Abroad

I was discharged from the air force on February 15, 1959, a few days before my twenty-second birthday. From there on I devoted all my efforts to three things: applying for admission to universities (all I needed was one admission, I told myself) in the United States for graduate studies; passing the Examination for Studying Abroad (held in early June); and securing a student visa from the U.S. Consulate in Taipei. All this had to be accomplished before August. Failing any one of the three would scuttle my entire plan.

There was a United States Information Service office not far from my home and it had a library. I spent a few days browsing through the catalogs of American universities. I checked their admission requirements, tuitions, the dates the schools started in the fall, etc. In the meantime, because Hsiao Tsung was still in uniform (his branch started late) and would not be discharged until June, I also collected information for him. In anticipation of studying abroad and making our given names easier to pronounce, we both decided to pick a common English name. Hsiao Tsung picked the name "David," while I picked "Stanley," from the book *Life with the Taylors*, in which there was a young fellow of that name. I wrote to several universities, including the ones David picked (he was stationed in the naval headquarters in Taipei, so he came home after work every day and signed the letters I wrote) requesting information and application materials. They all responded. After I sent off our applications, I got three admissions, from the University of Wisconsin-Madison, Ohio

University, and Oklahoma State University. David also got a few. One was from the University of Rhode Island. In addition to the admission, it also offered David an assistantship which would pay for tuition, plus a stipend. That decided for David which school he would attend. I was leaning toward going to Ohio University (I don't remember the reason why I picked that one). One objective was complete, namely, admission.

While I was busily preparing for my study abroad, I was constantly thinking about Shun Chih. I talked to Father one day to ask if it would be possible to use his influence (Father was the chief auditor representing the government's share in the bank) to get her transferred to Taipei, since she was working in a branch of the First Commerce Bank of Taiwan in Kaohsiung. He said he would talk to the general manager about it and that it should not be difficult, because there were many branches of the bank in Taipei and openings came up all the time. Of course, the most ideal one would be the one on Nanchang Street, about ten minutes' walk from our home.

Since I needed time during the day to study for the examination, a full-time job was not feasible. The examination for mechanical engineering majors consisted of four subjects: Chinese, English, civics, and thermodynamics. It did not feel right asking for an allowance from my parents after a year and half of pretty much being on my own while I was in the service. I found a part time job as a tutor for two high school students, working about eight hours a week. The students were a brother and sister, and I would tutor them on the subjects of trigonometry, plane geometry and some English. For that I was paid about NTD $650 per month, more than three times my lieutenant's pay. When their school was out for the summer, my hours were increased to twelve per week in the mornings. The pay came to NTD $1,000 per month. Apparently, their parents were happy about the help I had been giving their kids.

The rest of my time, besides writing frequently to Shun Chih, I devoted to studying the four subjects, specially English and thermodynamics. About a month before the big exams I enrolled in an English conversation class in the evenings taught by a Catholic nun. I dusted off the text on thermodynamics written by that same teacher who had taught me at TIT. A classmate had helped him to publish it by a process I have never seen in the United States. Using a stylus pen, he wrote the text on some special wax paper against a rough steel surface. Then he used a mimeographic process to print copies. We students paid only the cost of the labor and materials and the teacher did not get anything for his efforts. I believe his textbook covered the subject matter more in depth than most others. Unfortunately, due to the luggage limitation I did not bring the book with me when I came to the United States.

The day came for us to sit for the four-part exams, which took place at the National Taiwan University. Among the more than five thousand participants I only knew my brother, David, and three other classmates. Since there was no lecture hall or room big enough to have everyone under one roof, the exam was given in the auditorium and several large lecture halls. It took over a week for the many professors to grade all the test papers. Around mid-June, the examination commission announced the results. In addition to the old-fashioned way of announcement, by writing all the names of those who passed in calligraphy and posting it in a central location on campus, the commission also released the list to all the major newspapers in Taiwan. There were about 1,500 participants who passed the examination. I often wondered how the commissioners decided where to make the cut-off. I saw David's name and mine in the paper first, then I went to the university to really enjoy the results. I don't remember what place David's name was listed, but I counted my name to be around 300-ish of about 1,500. I was in the top twentieth percentile among those who passed. So, two objectives down!

Shortly after my exams, Father told me that Shun Chih would be transferred to the branch bank on Nanchang Street starting around mid-June. I was so thrilled that I called her long distance at her home that same evening, expecting that she already knew. In fact she had not been informed yet. Where would she stay? A few days later she told me that she had arranged to stay at the home of a childhood friend and grade-school classmate, a Miss Yu, sharing her room. Miss Yu's family knew Shun Chih's family as neighbors in the early years in Taipei. Her friend's home was about a fifteen-minute walk from the bank and they would not even charge her rent.

Before her arrival in Taipei, I told Father that I intended to propose to her. We would not rush to get married until my future was more certain. Father thought that was fine. He liked her, and besides, he also vaguely knew her father from many years ago.

I also picked out an English name—Nancy —for Shun Chih, planning to tell her about it after proposing. The day after her arrival, I took her out for the day. We went to Bitan (the name Bitan means "emerald lake") in the town of Hsindian, a suburb just a short bus ride from Taipei. We bought some precooked food and rented a row boat. I proposed to her on the boat. She accepted right away. Unfortunately, in the rush to plan the proposal, I neglected to buy any souvenir to commemorate the moment. I promised her that we would have a formal engagement dinner with both parents followed by a dancing party. We would both go shopping for the rings (one for each of us) but I could not promise her what kind of rings I could afford. She said she could help a little, as she had given most of her salary to her father during the past year for him to save. We also agreed that we would not get married right away. The bank where she was working had a strict rule: her job would be terminated upon marrying. So I needed a decent paying job before we could get married. I also suggested the name Nancy to her. She liked it.

That evening I gave Father a full report about the day's events. He was delighted. Knowing that we had no money, he asked me to invite Nancy over on Saturday afternoon. He would take us to Hengyang Street to shop for rings and he would pay for them.

Saturday, as planned, we took two pedicabs (one of the very few times we would ride in a pedicab—most of the time we took the city bus) to Hengyang Street. There were many jewelry stores lining both sides of the street. Father bought us one ring with several tiny diamonds for Nancy and a platinum ring for me. He also planned to have a formal dinner involving Nancy's parents. We requested that my uncle (he had been transferred to Banqiao as the head of the taxation bureau) be the official "match maker." We did not set the date of the dinner since Nancy's father was in Pingtung at the time, and I needed to officially ask his permission for our engagement.

In the meantime, I was busy with my plan to study abroad. I would need a passport for the student visa, but before I was allowed to apply for a passport, I needed a document from the military verifying my service record, and a certificate from the Department of Education certifying my passing of the foreign study exam. This all took time. Finally, everything was in place and I received my passport.

The biggest hurdle in getting a visa was the financial guarantee. The United States government did not want foreign students to take jobs away from American citizens. At the time, the financial guarantee needed for a year's study in the United States was $2,400 American. Even though David had been granted the assistantship, we thought it would be better if he also provided independent proof of the $2,400 guarantee to the U.S. Consulate. Father needed to come up with a total of $4,800 USD. At the time, the Taiwanese government was very much short of hard currency. For every student studying abroad, the government would only allow the exchange of up to $600 USD with the New Taiwan dollar. Father told us that he had been preparing for this day and we would be all right. The alternative for people needing U.S. dollars would be to buy them on the black market at an exchange rate of up to $44 NTD to an American dollar. The government's official exchange rate at the time was about $40 NTD for every American dollar.

On an early morning in late June, I brought my passport, the $2,400 USD bank draft made out to me, and the admission document from Ohio University to the U.S. Consulate office in Taipei to apply for a student visa. There were about 200 people already there at 7 AM. Rumor had it that only 15 to 20 percent of applicants got their visa on any given day. I got the necessary forms, filled them out, sat for a ten-minute written English composition, and got in line. Just a few minutes before noon, I thought they had forgotten about me. They had processed nearly everyone, even people who came after me. There was almost nobody left. They finally called me in. The vice-consul quickly read my composition, entitled

"My Favorite Dish." The only dish I could think of when writing was "Egg Stir Fried with Tomato," or maybe "Tomato Stir Fried with Egg." I can't remember which. To this day I still like both dishes and will cook them when Nancy does not object. I recall he commented that it sounded delicious. He then pointed to a tree outside of his office window and asked me how tall the tree was. I believe I replied that it was about twelve feet. In those days in Taiwan, we all used the metric system. I did not even know how tall twelve feet was in meters. In any case, he either liked my answers or was hungry and anxious to go to lunch, so I passed. He stamped my passport and signed it. It took less than five minutes. The date was June 25, 1959. This was three out of three. I was ready, able, and qualified to go to the United States of America to study.

With all the necessary procedures out of the way, I started to look into the cheapest way to get to America. It so happened that the merchant marine company owned by the government gave priority and discounts to students studying abroad. There was a brand new ship, weighing about 15,000 tons, scheduled to depart on her maiden voyage, bound for San Francisco, on August 3, 1959. I was able to book on it as one of a total of nine students for $228 USD, payable in New Taiwan Dollars.

With the last details settled, I turned my attention to our engagement. Nancy's father was on a business trip to Taipei around mid-July, so we went to see him in his hotel, across the street from the Taipei train station. I nervously presented him with our plans and asked his permission for our engagement. He happily approved. The only thing he emphasized was that I must have a steady job before we married. He obviously was not thinking about my going abroad. We set a date of July 24, 1959 (ten days before my scheduled departure) to have our formal engagement dinner. On that day Nancy's father would be back and would attend.

The engagement dinner was most impressive. Nancy was in a traditional Chinese *chipao* (long dress) and I was in a suit and tie. We went through the moves just like a formal Chinese wedding, bowing to each other, to the parents, to the "match makers," and to the witnesses officiating the ceremony. Unfortunately, Nancy's mother could not make the trip. We also sealed the engagement certificate. Later on our parents decided to change it into a marriage certificate, and registered it with the local government to change our status to married.

The day of my departure finally came. It was a clear, sunny day. Father, Shiao Ling, and Nancy went with me to Keelung to see me off. Mother did not come along as she did not like goodbyes. David had left Taiwan on August 1 from Kaohsiung. I accompanied him to Kaohsiung to see him off. Nancy and I had so much to say to each other, but as the time came we could say nothing. Finally I stood on the bow with tears running down my cheeks and saw Nancy dabbing her eyes. We waved to each other until I could not see her anymore.

CHAPTER IX:

Crossing the Pacific Ocean

There were only nine passengers. I had no idea what the crew size was. We all were students going to study in the United States, three girls and six guys. I learned that the freighter normally had twelve berths for passengers. But on this trip there were three seaman apprentices, hence there were only nine of us. During the first night, as we headed northeast toward Japan across the East China Sea, the sea got rough because there was a typhoon in that region. After dinner, served in the dining room, I stayed in my bunk and the ship rocked me to sleep. The next day when I got up, the sea was a lot rougher than the night before, almost like the time when I went from Hong Kong to Taiwan across the Taiwan Strait. I walked to the deck and threw up on the side of the ship. After the ship cleared southern Japan and headed into the Pacific Ocean, the sea was considerably calmer. At meal time I was usually the only one in the dining room eating. This was pretty much the same every day for most of the trip. I wondered how the girls survived the trip, because I seldom saw them in the dining room eating.

Occasionally, when there was a very calm day, the girls emerged from their cabin. We all sat in the dining room and talked about the lives we had left behind. There was a girl named Lin, who told us she had a boyfriend who had left Taiwan the previous year for the United States. They had almost become engaged before he left, but did not go through with it. They believed true love did not require such formality. Besides, there were many cases in which engaged couples broke up after a time of separation. Six months after her boyfriend got to the United States, he met another girl and stopped writing to Lin. She was quite bitter. When she saw the ring I was wearing and found out that I was engaged, she laughed at me. She guaranteed that I would be forgetting all about Nancy within a year. She believed that when it came to love, no man could be trusted. I told her that that might be true for other men, but not me. There were no shipboard romances between the rest of the guys and the three girls, because they were all seasick most of the time.

I was alone most of the trip, so I had a lot of time to contemplate my future. I remembered I had told Nancy that my plan was to spend two years completing my master's degree, do a year of practical training, hopefully save some money and then to come home at the end of the third year. When I returned, we would get married. In the meantime Nancy would move into my parents' home, because Shiao Ling (later on my sister picked the English name "Shirley," naturally) would be the only one at home (and she would be going to America after a year anyway). Nancy did move in with my parents after Shirley left. With my parents' encouragement Nancy quit the bank job and went to the Mingzhuan College for Commerce, an all-girls college at that time.

Because the freighter was empty, it carried 3,000 tons of sea water, according to one crewman, just so it did not float too high above the water. Onboard, there was nowhere to go. I did visit the ship's bridge once, but it did not leave me too big of an impression.

Since there was nothing to do on board, I made use of the time to study one of my weaker subjects, mathematics. My teacher had just started differential equations before our semester ran out. I slowly went through the textbook I had brought with me, and then picked up speed. I tried to do as many exercise problems as possible. From time to time, I would write some short paragraphs to be sent to Nancy after I arrived in America.

After about seventeen days at sea, I had pretty much finished the differential equations book. The ship pulled into San Francisco on August 19, 1959. I picked up my two suitcases and got off the ship. Luckily, the Greyhound bus station was not far from the dock.

I bought a ticket from San Francisco all the way to Athens, Ohio. The bus company allowed passengers to make as many stops as one wanted, for any length of time. I had plans to stop in Iowa City to see a friend of one of my colleagues from military service in Pingtung. This friend of a friend was attending graduate school at the University of Iowa.

I checked my suitcases with the bus company. Carrying a small bag, I walked the streets around the bus station before departing San Francisco. The city was kind of hilly, with streets going up and down. I was getting a little hungry. I stopped in front of a store, looking through the glass front doors, I saw people sitting at a counter in the back eating, so I walked in thinking it was a restaurant. There were no other tables or chairs inside so I approached the counter. A lady behind the counter asked me something I could not understand. I assumed she was asking what I wanted. Looking up I saw the picture of a bowl of soup and some crackers, so I just pointed at it and smiled. She brought me the soup and crackers and asked something else I could not understand. I just shook my head and she walked away. When I finished the soup and crackers I really needed something more. But I could not express myself properly so I did not ask for anything else. When she brought me the bill and said something, I pointed at the apples under a glass cover. She handed me an apple. I took out a dollar and she gave me some change. I found out that the apple was 10 cents. The whole bill including the soup and crackers was less than 60 cents. At the rate of NTD $40 to one American dollar, that "lunch" came to about NTD $24. That would be enough for Nancy and me to have two meals each. I stuffed the apple in my bag and boarded the bus. I would snack on the apple later.

For the next two days and nights, the bus rolled on. I had sweet rolls and milk for breakfast, soup and crackers for both lunch and dinner, with apples as supplements. When the bus stopped at Iowa City in the morning, I took my suitcases and got off the bus. In a short while, the friend of my colleague during the service arrived in a rickety old car. He stopped the car in front of the station, and introduced himself. Obviously, my colleague had not failed me. He had written to his friend and timed my arrival perfectly. I was so happy to see a friendly Chinese face who spoke Chinese after two days on the bus. I put the suitcases in the trunk of his car. It took a few slams to close the trunk. I climbed into the passenger side. Apparently the car did not have shock absorbers (I ought to know since I was a "graduate" of a driving summer camp). When we went over a grade crossing, the front wheels of the car hit a bump. The car bounced so high my head hit the ceiling. The friend apologized and said that he should have it fixed. I knew he was just saying that to be polite and would not actually fix it.

This friend rented a kitchenette with another student who happened to be away for the summer. For supper, he cooked a pot of rice, boiled a chicken, and opened a can of something. I had not had rice since I got off the ship and had been hungry for the two days on the bus. I stuffed myself with the rice and the delicious chicken with soy sauce.

After dinner he took me around the school sightseeing. We talked about our mutual friend, about his serving the second eighteen months in ROTC, and his failure to pass the studying-abroad examination for a third time. I slept soundly that night since I had not gotten much sleep on the bus. When I woke up the next morning, the sun was already up. I lay in bed and looked out the wide-open front door. We had not even closed the door before we went to sleep. The friend assured me that it was very safe near the university and that he always left the front door open, especially during the summer since the house had no air conditioning. I had never heard of an air conditioner then.

Breakfast was the leftover rice, cooked into congee served with the leftover chicken and some other stuff. There was another bus coming by mid-morning. The friend took me back to the station and we said goodbye. The next two days and two nights seemed to pass by quickly. My friend had taught me how to order sandwiches at the lunch counter, so I was not that hungry during the remaining trip. I was spending more money than expected.

Chapter X:

The Ohio University Days

The Greyhound bus delivered me to Athens, Ohio the home of Ohio University, on a weekday (Friday, if I recall correctly). This was fortunate, because offices would be open. After I claimed my luggage I thought about where I should go. I had not planned this far ahead before I left home. Finally I decided that since the admission was sent by the graduate school, I should go to the graduate school office. I did not know where the graduate school office was. Later I found out that it was only a short walk from the bus station. With two suitcases, I could not walk far. I hired a taxi and with some difficulty the driver finally understood where I wanted to go. The driver dropped me with my suitcases near the front door of the graduate school office. I walked in with the letter of admission in hand and showed it to a person (I can't remember whether it was a man or a woman) at the front desk. It took me a while with my broken English to explain that I had just arrived on campus from the Republic of China, Taiwan. I was sure the clerk had never heard of Taiwan until I mentioned the name Formosa.

It was summertime, and most offices had skeleton staffs, and it was a Friday afternoon to boot. So what would the clerk do with me? After a few phone calls, which seemed to take an eternity, we finally found a solution. I was sent to one of the dormitories that housed foreign students, at least through the weekend. Then someone from the office helped me with one of the suitcases and walked me to the dormitory (I forget the building's name). I was introduced to a lady (probably in her mid-forties with heavy makeup) who was in charge of all the foreign students who stayed on campus during recesses and holidays. The person who took me there left some instructions for that lady about me that I did not understand. She nodded, smiled at me, and called me "honey" (I did know the meaning of the term). She came over toward me, grabbed my shoulder, and started to hug me. That made me very uncomfortable. I believed that she sensed that, so she stopped and picked up one of my suitcases and led me to a room that had two beds. One was occupied and she told me that this would where I would be staying until school started. I would have my meals at the dining hall with the other students but I had to work for my meals. When dinner time came, I just followed my roommate to the dining hall to eat.

We were early for dinner. When we got there, we met the head dietician. I gave her my name and I explained to her that I had just arrived this afternoon. Since I was new she went through the routine about our serving the football players first before we ate. Soon the players came in. They were big guys. My impression was that the smallest one was a couple inches taller and at least 20 kilograms (44 pounds) heavier than I. My roommate told me later on that these players were on the school team and this was their summer training camp before classes began. The first game was usually played after Labor Day against a regional university. One day during their practice, my roommate and I decided to watch them. I thought they were playing the same kind of "football" as I had back at TIT. It turned out they were using an olive-shaped, not round, leather ball. Instead of kicking the ball around, the player tried to run with it. I had seen this kind of game played before in Taiwan. We called it the "Olive Ball." The round "football" was called "soccer" and played mostly in England, Europe, Asia, Latin America, and elsewhere.

Over the weekend, there was not much for me to do, so I unpacked the suitcase which held most of the dirty laundry accumulated during the trip. I asked my roommate what to do with our dirty laundry. He showed me the laundry room, full of box-shaped washing machines. He patiently explained to me how to operate the machines by inserting a quarter, and how to buy detergent from a vending machine for a dime, and how much detergent to put into a load of wash. When the wash was done, I could spend another quarter to put the wash in a dryer. I was so excited. From now on I would always have clean clothes to wear. I did not have to spend hours washing my clothes. I also could not imagine where I would have found long bamboo poles or ropes to hang up the washing to dry.

When Monday came, the lady in charge of us foreign students told me that I probably should check in with my department and that I would receive further instructions from them. She even gave me a map of the campus and showed me the building where the department of mechanical engineering was.

It was a short walk to the departmental office, and the chairman of the department happened to be in, according to his secretary. I introduced myself to Professor Paul H. Black. With my broken English, I tried to tell him as much as possible about myself. He was delighted to see me and was very patient in listening to my story. He told me the department had just started the graduate program a couple of years ago, granting master's degrees only. At the present time there were seven graduate students and I would be the only foreign graduate student. There were other undergraduate students from Hong Kong, whom I met later on.

During our first meeting I asked Professor Black if it was possible for me to apply for a graduate tuition scholarship. He said it was quite possible, because the graduate college wanted to help young programs such as ours. All the other six (American) students had tuition scholarships. He sent me to the graduate college to see the dean, Dr. D. R. Clippinger. As a matter of fact he called ahead for me to make an appointment. I knew from Friday where the graduate school was, so I hurried over. Dr. Clippinger received me right away. After a short interview, he told me I merely needed to fill out an application as a formality and he would grant me the graduate tuition scholarship. A year of tuition was about $780. Add that to room and board of around $750 for two semesters and by next summer, I would have spent roughly $1,500. This would have taken a big bite out of the savings I had brought with me. I was so excited and happy to receive the scholarship that I immediately wrote to my parents and Nancy.

At the end of summer, before school started, I got a check for $4.50 for serving the football players and working in the kitchen, less the cost of my meals. I was told that the money was based on my hourly pay of $0.75.

Before classes started, I moved into Tiffany Hall, which housed mostly upperclassmen. I requested and was given a single room since I needed all the private time I could get to study. Prior to my leaving Taiwan, I printed up 100 name cards (or business cards) with just my name, Stanley S. H. Chen. I typed "Graduate Student" below my name and put a card on my door, as I believed I would get more respect from fellow residents as a graduate student. It seemed to work, because I was never bothered by anyone. Shortly after school started the undergraduate students from Hong Kong found out that I had a single room. Some of them came to my room around 10 PM one evening. They brought over a pot and a hot plate and wanted to cook rice and other dishes. At first I welcomed them, because I craved rice and company. Eventually this became an everyday event which really cut into my study time.

In addition to the undergraduate students from Hong Kong from the neighboring dormitory, there was another Chinese graduate student, James Yao. He had also graduated from Taipei Institute of Technology, but in electrical engineering and two years earlier. James told me there was another student from TIT, also in electrical engineering who had graduated the same year as I did. His name was Wai Kai Chen. He did not live in the dorm. He rented a room from a professor and ate his meals at local eateries. I met Wai Kai later on, and recalled that I had met him back at TIT when he came to meetings of the Zhejiang Province Friendship Association. I also remembered that he had a twin brother, Wai Fah. They graduated with class 27 (I was in class 26) of the Junior High School at the National Normal University. Wai Kai took the same educational route as I did. Wai Fah went on to senior high and the National Taiwan University. He came to the United States two years later.

I realized that having a single room was a big mistake because the nightly visit by the Hong Kong students. Toward the end of the fall semester I went to talk with the resident head, a graduate student, and informed him that I wanted to move to a double room. The reason I gave him was that I wanted more opportunity to learn both the English language and the American culture. He understood and reassigned me to a double room. My roommate's name was Dale Walters, and his family lived in Dayton, Ohio. He was a nice and easygoing guy, and we got along very well. During Easter break, he invited me to visit his family and I even went with his family to attend Easter Sunday church service. As a result, the late-night visits and cooking stopped. Dale was majoring in business, I believe, so he did not have to study much. He was not bothered that I studied all the time.

In February, I received a package from home. It had some canned food and clothes, among other items. I opened a can of pickled vegetables, which I had not had for a long time. Dale was closely watching me, anxious to find out what Chinese people ate. The smell from the pickled vegetables made him immediately hold his nose and jump out the window. Good thing our room was on the first floor; otherwise he might have suffered a serious injury. From then on I was always careful not to open cans of Chinese food when he was in the room.

After I became more comfortable with my English, I asked the resident head if it would be possible for me to work at the front desk helping to man the switchboard. Since not many people liked to work the Saturday afternoon and evening shifts, he agreed, paying me $0.75 an hour. My duties were answering the phone when calls came in and dispatching them to the proper floor, since we had no phones in our rooms. I was also to check out equipment, such as the limited supply of books, magazines, chess sets, and playing cards. During the first few weeks, unless the calls were for Smith or Jones, I had to ask the caller to spell out the name, at least twice. I wrote them down and checked the resident lists before I patched them through. It seemed that nobody complained. I worked from about four in the afternoon to midnight, earning $6 per week. Later on I also picked up some hours on Sunday afternoons.

I had some difficulty in class at the beginning of the semester. As I was copying down the writing on the blackboard, I would often miss what the professor was saying, not that I could totally understand the lectures anyway. After a couple of months I got used to their lectures and became a lot more proficient. I took five classes, fifteen credit hours. Thirty-six credit hours were required to complete the master's degree with six hours allowed for the master's theses. At the end of the semester I had earned four A's and one B, not bad for the first semester. I did well in Advanced Strength of Materials. Sometimes I went into the testing laboratory, which was a part of the undergraduate level of the Strength of Materials class. Toward the end of the semester I asked the professor if I could grade the lab reports for him for the next semester. He agreed, since I was already there observing. Sometimes I even volunteered to help the students in answering some of their questions. The grading job would pay me $150 for the semester.

So beginning in the spring semester I started to grade lab reports. I usually did the grading on Saturday afternoons and evenings during the time I was working at the front desk switchboard. With my two jobs, I made close to $250 for the four months of spring semester, which came to about NTD $10,000, or NTD $2,500 per month. Compared to my classmates in Taiwan—a starting salary as a junior engineer was around NTD$750 per month—I was making it big time.

I took another fifteen credit hours during the spring semester, which left only the six hours for the master's thesis, so I believed I could finish my degree by the end of the summer. I consulted with Professor Black about continuing my graduate studies, since Ohio University did not offer a PhD in mechanical engineering. I was hoping he could recommend a university for me to apply to. He advised me that since I came from Taiwan and had been in school all my life, it would be beneficial for me to work in industry for a few years to gain some practical experience before continuing. He even took the time to go through a catalog on "College Placement" (I can't remember the name of the pamphlet for sure). The catalog contained companies advertising job openings. He identified several possible employers, one of which was the A. O. Smith Corporation in

Milwaukee, Wisconsin. I fired off letters, a shoe box full, to the hiring firms. I did not have time to type individual letters, so I used the only means (in those days) to produce a large quantity of form letters: the "ditto master" technology. I learned later that this type of letter would most likely be immediately discarded by the people upon receiving. But I got a response from the A. O. Smith Corporation.

Most of the letters I sent received no response. The few replies all said they did not have an opening for someone with my qualifications. But sometime during the summer, the A. O. Smith Corporation responded and offered me an interview for an opening in their plastics research laboratory. I dusted off my tailor-made suit and went to the interview. On that particular day they also interviewed an American job candidate. What struck me about my fellow applicant was that his hands were at the end of his upper arms. He did not have forearms. He must have been interviewing with a different department, because after we jointly met with the personnel representative, I did not see him again except when we shared a taxi cab back to the airport. I don't think he was hired.

Figure 4: At Ohio University, fall 1959.

During the interview, I talked to the lab director, Mr. Ken Charter; mechanical engineering supervisor Mr. Fred Pflederer; and a Dr. Ken Blanchard, director of the research division of the company. I also was interviewed by a Dr. Robert Bodine, a graduate of the University of Wisconsin-Madison, a man of few words. They explained to me that I was being interviewed for a position working on development of a reinforced plastic pipe. Mr. Pflederer specifically mentioned that the Theory of Elasticity class I had taken (and got an A in) was very much of interest to him. Fortunately, he did not know that I had a very marginal professor. Although we used the textbook written by S. Timoshenko, we did not get much beyond the third chapter. I suspect that this was the limit of the instructor's knowledge in the subject. Later on, at the University of Wisconsin, I retook the same class.

About three weeks before my thesis oral defense, I heard from the A. O. Smith Corporation. They offered me the position of junior experimental engineer, with a monthly salary of $600. I was very excited. At the same time I also received offers of an instructor position at a salary of $550 per month from Eaton College in Pennsylvania, and an admission from Lehigh University for a PhD program. Eaton College was only a short drive from Lehigh. I had applied to these schools before I consulted with Professor Black. Now I had to think about which way to go. Trying to consult with my parents and Nancy in Taiwan was out of the question, because a round-trip letter would take two to three weeks. I had to make the decision to accept one offer and reject the other two. I remembered that I promised Nancy that I would work for a year, save some money, and go back to Taiwan to marry her. PhD study would take three to five years or longer if I had a full-time job. So finally I came to the easy (and best) decision to work at the A. O. Smith Corporation. I broke the news to Professor Black. He was very pleased that he had really helped me. I also wrote letters to my parents and Nancy as soon as my decision was made. In their return mail, they all agreed that I had made the right choice.

**Figure 5: Graduation with MSME from
Ohio University, August 1960.**

My thesis and oral defense was the only thing left to complete. The title of my thesis was "An Analysis of the Harmonic Drive," an idea I picked up from the February 1960 issue of *Product Engineering* at the library. Since I did not originate the idea, I tried, with my limited abilities, to do a reasonably thorough analysis. I wrote my thesis out in long hand and handed to Professor Black to edit. He generously applied his red pen, and his wife even typed it up in triplicate for me at a very low cost.

I wrote back to the A. O. Smith Corporation after my thesis orals. I accepted their offer and would report to work the day after Labor Day. The reason for the two-week delay was that Shirley was scheduled to arrive around the end of August. She had also decided to study for her master's degree at Ohio University. I had about two weeks of "vacation" while waiting for her to help her get settled. It was the most relaxed and rested I felt during the whole year.

At the beginning of summer, James, Wai Kai, and I decided we ought to rent a house instead of continuing to live in the dormitories. We found a small, two-level furnished house on Race Street. It had a living room, kitchen, and one good-sized bedroom. We rented the upstairs, and the downstairs was rented by a single woman. We had separate entrances. Since I was only staying for the summer, I chose to sleep on the couch in the living room. James and I did most of the cooking and Wai Kai was the dishwasher. We were very happy about the arrangement.

During that two-week vacation, the most pressing chore was buying a car, because the company told me that I needed to have a car. My assigned workplace was a testing laboratory in the outskirts of Milwaukee and the city bus would not go there. After arriving in Ohio, I had sent most of my money to David for him to keep for Shirley's financial guarantee. Now I needed some money to buy a car, and to meet living expenses in Milwaukee before I received my first paycheck. David sent me about $900. I used $600 to buy a 1955 Ford. During the summer, I talked the only student from Hong Kong who owned a car into letting me practice driving for about an hour in exchange for some tutoring in mathematics. I already knew how to drive for the most part. I went to take the driver's license test and passed.

The day before Labor Day, I was like an ant on a hot plate waiting for David to show up. He had also bought a car and planned to drive out to see me in Athens. Shirley was not to arrive until almost three weeks later it turned out. Around mid-day on Labor Day, after David had still not shown up, I told James and Wai Kai that I had to leave. It would take about ten hours to drive to Milwaukee, and I planned to stop overnight somewhere in between. I had promised the A. O. Smith Corporation that I would report to work on the day after Labor Day. I did not want to be late. I found out later that a few hours after I left, David arrived in Athens.

On the day Shirley arrived in the United States, her plane landed in San Francisco. But her connecting flight to Columbus, Ohio was at the Oakland airport. Apparently the travel agent in Taiwan who arranged the flight did not know or neglected to mention this detail to her. Fortunately, on the plane, she talked to another student and they realized the complication. Since that student had a family in San Francisco and they were to meet his plane and drive him to Oakland, Shirley hitched a ride with them to the Oakland airport.

Wai Kai and James had no car. The day before Shirley left Taiwan she received a letter from James saying that she should take the bus to Athens on her own. It was about a two and a half hour ride. Upon her arrival in Athens she took a taxi to 9 Race Street. When she arrived the house was locked. She and her luggage sat on the porch and waited. That must have been the longest and most horrible time of her life. It so happened that the lady downstairs, Mabel, came up, and they found the back door open. They moved her luggage inside and Mabel invited Shirley to wait with her downstairs. Shortly afterward James and Wai Kai came home. Since they had no idea when she would arrive, they had gone grocery shopping. The very first letter Shirley wrote home reported all this. I received a letter from Mother criticizing me for abandoning my own poor sister. As a matter of fact, no amount of explanation I wrote would satisfy her. For many years, whenever the subject came up, she would chew me out anew. Finally, after forty-seven years, Wai Kai verified that Shirley's actual arrival day, a Sunday, was almost three weeks after I went to work and one week after the fall semester had already started. I explained to Mother again about the timing of it all. Her response was that since this was all so long ago there was no need to continue talking about it. She would not admit that I did not deserve all the blame she had assigned throughout the years.

When I left Athens, I told Wai Kai and James that I would come back to visit them during the Christmas holidays. James begged me to bring some of the famous Schlitz beer from Milwaukee when I came back. When Christmas time arrived, in order to save some time after work on Friday, I bought a case of beer the night before and stored it in the trunk of my car. When I finally got to Athens, about midnight, I proudly opened the trunk and was hit by an overwhelming beer smell. I totally forgot that the overnight temperature was in the teens, and half the glass bottles had burst. So much for the famous beer. We still had a few unbroken ones to enjoy.

Chapter XI:

Working for A. O. Smith Corporation and Marriage

The day after Labor Day 1960, I arrived in Milwaukee, Wisconsin just before noon. I went directly to the office, left my luggage in the car, and reported for work. I spent most of the afternoon filling out paperwork. I was officially employed. They told me to leave work a little early to find a place to stay. Someone gave me the address of the YMCA in the downtown area and I got there without any problems. Shortly after I checked into my room, I heard a knock on the door and opened it. David stood there with the widest grin on his face. He had finally found me. David told me that James told him that I would be staying in a YMCA. When he got into the city he stopped at a telephone booth, checked the directory, and found two YMCAs. One was in the downtown area, so he decided to give that one the first try. We stayed there for a couple of nights.

The next day, as soon as he found out that I drove all the way from Ohio without car insurance, he went out and found an insurance agency and bought the minimum liability insurance for me. The third day, while I was at work, he drove around the neighborhood close to the A. O. Smith Corporation and found a family with a spare front room and rented it for me at $50 per month. We moved in after work. The room had a double bed, a desk and chair, and a small refrigerator. The landlord even provided a small hot plate and warned us that it was for heating water and stuff only, not for serious cooking. I was all set. David was a big help.

After dinner on Friday, since this was the first time we had gotten together since we both left Taiwan, we decided to call our parents to tell them how we were. With permission from the landlord and a promise that we would reimburse the cost of the international long distance, we made the call. It took a while for the operator to patch us through a couple of interchanges. After the operator told Mother it was long distance from the United States, Mother went silent for a while. It took a good minute to convince her we were who we said we were. She sounded frightened. She repeatedly asked us if we were all right. After repeated assurances that we were all right and insistences that we just wanted to hear her and Father's voices, she started to chew us out for frightening her and wasting money on the useless long-distance call. It must have taken her three minutes to calm down. Father took over the conversation and asked some relevant questions. He congratulated me for finishing my master's degree and getting a job in only one year. He was surprised that I was already working, since they had not received the most recent letter I had written. The phone call took about nine minutes, and we paid the landlord $36.

On Saturday, we decided to venture out to Chicago, the big city, for sightseeing. It was about 100 miles away. It would take about a couple of hours one way. After we drove around the city, visited Chinatown, and had dinner, we decided to stop in a strip joint to see what it was like. There were half-naked girls dancing on a stage. Before we knew it, two girls sat down on either side of us. One asked David if we would buy them a drink. Before he even understood their question, he kind of nodded his head. Quickly two tall glasses of clear liquid (they called it champagne) were set in front of the girls. The person who brought them over wanted $20, $10 for each drink. We did not have much of a choice and did not know how to argue with the guy, so David paid. We stayed about half an hour. There was nothing much to see. We decided to leave before they sicked other girls on us.

On the way home I drove first, then I got sleepy. I let David take over and soon I felt the ride was kind of bumpy. I opened my eyes to find the car was weaving between the pavement and the highway shoulder. Now that I had had a little catnap, I took over and drove the rest of the way to our rented room.

Sunday was a leisurely day. We drove along the street bordering the shore of Lake Michigan and stopped to enjoy 10-cent soft ice cream cones. We pooled all our remaining paper money between us, and it came to under $30. When David first arrived in Milwaukee we had several hundred dollars between us. But in those few days we had been spending a lot for motel rooms, the YMCA, prepaid rent, car insurance, the long-distance call and the champagne in Chicago, plus our meals. Since I still had a loaf of bread and some cold cuts, and David had a long way to go back to Rhode Island, I gave all the money to him, except an old silver dollar that I had bought from a student at Tiffany Hall when I was working at the switchboard.

The early part of the week after David left was fine. After Wednesday I started to watch the gas gauge of my Ford. The loaf of bread was getting shorter because it had to serve me for all three meals each day. On Friday, I sat at my desk and wondered how I was going to survive the weekend and the following week, if the company only pays once a month at the end of the month. There was a guy, T. Tao Chiao, in the chemical engineering group, who I might be able to borrow $10 from to tide me over another week. He was working at the main building where I had interviewed. I hesitated about calling him, because I had only met him once for a couple of minutes. I never did call because of how embarrassed I felt.

About mid-afternoon, my technician, Mr. Tom Brownell, came into my office and handed me an envelope. I saw he had other envelopes in his hand, so I knew that must be a paycheck. I quickly opened the envelope as soon as he turned his back. Sure enough it was my pay for the two weeks since I started. By starting on the day after Labor Day, I earned the pay for the Labor Day holiday as well. After all the deductions the net of the check was still more than $180. I was so relieved. Our workday was 7:30 AM to 4:30 PM with one hour for lunch. Since our lab was on the outskirts of the city, we were allowed to take a half-hour lunch and knock off at 4 PM. Since banks stayed open till 5, I headed directly to a bank in my neighborhood, a Marshall and Isley Bank. I opened an account, deposited my pay, and took out $20 for spending money. From that time on, I would never be short of cash in my wallet again. The first order of business was filling up my car. At 23 cents a gallon, a tank of gas cost about $3. I went to my room, freshened up, and went to the Toy Chinese Restaurant, where I really treated myself. After spending $3 including a tip, I was really stuffed. Then I went grocery shopping.

I really enjoyed my work and got along well with my co-workers, mostly technicians, and my boss, Mr. Fred Pflederer. He had a BSME degree. In order to quickly improve my English proficiency I asked all the people around me to correct me on my pronunciation and grammar on the spot. That would be the only way to learn, and I would not feel embarrassed. Most of them abided by my request.

After about three months, Fred told me that he and the lab director Mr. Charter had a favorable preliminary review (normally it would be every six months) of my performance. They had recommended to the company higher-ups to apply to the Immigration and Naturalization Services (INS) for "permanent residence" status for me under the third preference (engineers and scientists) rule. I immediately wrote to Nancy to tell her the good news. I would have a good chance to get a green card. Then she could come to the United States, instead of my going home, and we could get married here.

After a couple months renting that family's spare room, I looked around and found a one-room furnished efficiency apartment on a second floor. It had a small kitchen with a refrigerator in an alcove for $5 more in rent ($55 per month), so I moved in. Now I could learn to cook for myself, which would be much more convenient and cheaper than eating out. One time I even roasted a duck with soy sauce. What a tasty dish! It was almost like the duck our maid cooked at home. I even invited some Chinese students over to sample it. I stayed at this apartment for about a year before Nancy came.

Further advanced studies were always on my mind. There are two large universities in Milwaukee. One is the University of Wisconsin-Milwaukee (UWM) and the other one is Marquette University, both near downtown. During the spring semester of 1961, I signed up for a complex variables class at Marquette (which is on Wisconsin Avenue). After only one week of class, I was sent to San Antonio, Texas for two weeks to monitor field-testing of experimental reinforced plastic pipes. The reason the tests were conducted in Texas was that the product was aimed at the oil field market. Many of the oil pipes were installed above ground and subjected to sun and the weather. The tests were contracted out to the Southwest Research Institute. I enjoyed the experience but constantly worried about my missed classes, because complex variables was my weakest subject. I tried to study as much as possible, but the exercises in the book were very hard. Quite often I did not even know how to start them. After I returned to Milwaukee and rejoined the class, the instructor announced that we would have our first test a week later. Naturally I failed the test, getting a fifty-nine out of 100, near the bottom of the class. After some agonizing debate I decided to drop the class without penalty (possible within the first month of class). This would prove to be the only class I ever dropped.

During the fall semester of 1961, I registered for a class at Marquette and another one at the UWM, since both schools had a policy that limited full-time employed students to only one class per semester. I also found out that if I got a B or better, the company would reimburse my tuition. I managed to get A's in both classes and even received a letter of congratulation from the vice-president of the research division, Mr. Robert McGinn.

In late spring 1961, I was notified by the local INS office that my company-sponsored application for permanent residence status was approved, pending quota availability. It could be another six months or a year or more before final approval. I was so excited I wrote Nancy about the good news. At the time she was already at the Ming Chuan Commercial College for Girls and had moved into my parents' home. If I had to wait for two years for the green card, she would have time to graduate, since she had started at the three-year college in 1960. I started to think about ways that Nancy could come to the United States to get married, in case the final approval came early. I retained an attorney (paying him a $50 retainer) to look into the laws regarding situations similar to mine. As with most attorneys, this guy worked at a snail's pace. Around January 1962, INS notified me that I made the quota and my application was finally approved. They sent me the coveted green card.

I moved from the one-room efficiency to a one-bedroom unfurnished apartment in late summer 1961, in order to be closer to the universities. I also wanted a bigger place, after having received the preliminary approval for the green card. The apartment had a living room and kitchen. Regarding furniture, a friend suggested the Goodwill Industries store, from which I bought a twin bed, a dining table set, a couch, lamps, and other odds and ends.

Peter Chien (Jin Sheng), a classmate from TIT, came to Milwaukee in September 1961. He had injured one of his knees on board the ship over. He had an admission from the University of Wisconsin-Madison, but he felt that he couldn't begin school in his current physical condition. So he stayed with me. He elected to sleep on the couch. He hoped his knee got better and he could go to UW during the spring. Since his injury, he had never been seen by a physician, so I took him to see a doctor. The doctor took an x-ray to make sure he did not have any broken bones, and put a cast on his leg to immobilize the knee joint to help with the recovery. Peter was totally bored when I went to work during the day and to school in the evening. William Marr, also a TIT classmate going to Marquette University for his master's degree on an assistantship, came over from time to time to alleviate Peter's boredom.

One day, apparently out of frustration, Peter tore off his cast with a kitchen knife. He thought the cast was inhibiting his mobility. Since he did not feel any pain in the knee joint, he wanted to go out to find a job. When I came home from work and saw what had happened, I was amazed and angry. There were plaster bits everywhere. I cleaned it up and did not say anything. The next day, I noticed that his leg was very weak and he could not walk without his crutch. I told him that he had a choice. Either I could take him back to the doctor to put on another cast, which would cost additional money that he did not have, or he needed to be really patient and not move around while waiting for the knee to heal. He did not want to go back to the doctor.

Upon receiving a green card, I immediately wrote to my parents and Nancy about the news. I also called the attorney to ask him if he had come up with any information. He said he had not. In the meantime in Taiwan, Mother found out that in order to be considered legally married all we needed was a duly sealed marriage certificate registered with the local government. We would then be declared husband and wife. Mother contacted Nancy's father, who thought it was an excellent idea. Since we had our formal engagement, the actual marriage process would just be another formality. According to the custom in Taiwan, after a formal engagement such as ours, the future bride and groom would start to live together before marriage. But all the parents and witnesses agreed to seal our marriage certificate just the same. Mother took the certificate to the local government, had it registered, and sent a copy of the household registry to me. I sent it on to the Consulate General of the Republic of China in Chicago with my passport in order to amend my status to "Married." In the meantime I sent a copy of my INS approval letter to Nancy, to be taken to the U.S. Consulate General in Taipei to get her immigration visa. Her passport already listed my name as her husband. I quickly called my attorney to stop his work in this matter. He agreed and told me I did not owe him any more money.

In early 1962, I was getting ready for Nancy's arrival. I needed to clean up the apartment and get a new double bed for the bedroom. I talked to William to ask if he could host Peter for a few months until my guest was well enough to use the Wisconsin admission. William agreed but indicated that he would not be spending a lot of time with Peter either. He had started dating Jane Liu (they were married in September, Nancy was the maid of honor and I was the best man) and besides, he had his own studies to attend to. So it was settled. Peter moved to William's place around mid-March.

It was March 1962 and most of Nancy's paperwork was in place, except the visa to immigrate to the U.S. Once the visa was issued, there was a window of six months to use it. After six months the visa would expire and she would have to reapply. The question was whether Nancy should finish the spring semester or wait another year to finish college. I was all for her coming right away. She could always apply to and attend college in the United States. So she went to the U.S. Consulate to get her visa. Since all my friends and co-workers knew I was engaged, when Nancy showed up, I would have to have a formal marriage ceremony, otherwise we would have lots of explaining to do. I started the wedding preparations. As soon as I knew her arrival date, I set the wedding for the next day. Father recommended having the wedding day a week after her arrival just in case the flight got delayed.

I borrowed a wedding dress from the wife of a friend, since she and Nancy were about the same size. I rented a union hall for the afternoon of Saturday, April 14, 1962. I had catered food and a keg of beer for the reception. There were over ninety people who showed up and everyone seemed to have a good time. David flew in. He was the only relative at the wedding. After an early dinner with the leftovers from the wedding reception, we drove off to some unknown destination and left the apartment to David for the night. We ended up checked in at a motel at the edge of town. On Sunday afternoon we took David to the airport. We ran into a traffic jam and I had to cut through a gas station to get to a side street near the airport. He was barely in time to catch his flight home.

**Figure 6: David (left), Nancy, and I in our
apartment after the wedding.**

I did not take any classes during the spring of 1962 on account
of the wedding. I took one class at UWM in the fall. Nancy did not
have much to do during the day, so I suggested she read some simple
English books to help her with the language. We would walk to a

neighborhood supermarket, an A & P, to buy groceries. We each would carry a bag and walk home to our apartment. On weekends we usually drove to the park along Lake Michigan and bought 10-cent soft ice cream cones. I also took Nancy to the park to let her practice her driving skills. It was over five years since she had last sat behind the steering wheel of a car. She relearned quickly and passed the tough Milwaukee city driving test on her first try.

Figure 7: Formal wedding picture, April 1962.

In late August 1962, I took a week's vacation and we drove to White Plains, New York to attend David and Shirley's double wedding. Shirley was to marry Wai Kai, and David was marrying Gwendyline, whom he had met while he was in Taiwan. I was representing Father to give Shirley away. Nancy had her hands full trying to help both Shirley and Gwendyline get ready. Both couples were married on September 1, 1962.

Since going to graduate school remained on my mind, I applied to the University of Illinois at Champaign-Urbana (UI) to study for my PhD. The reason I picked UI was that Shirley and Wai Kai were studying there after they had graduated with their master's degrees from Ohio University. I got an admission from the aeronautical engineering department, along with a teaching assistantship. In early summer I submitted my resignation through the proper channels at my company. giving them my reasons for leaving.

Shortly after that, I received a letter from a Miss Ham in charge of foreign student admissions at UI. In the letter she stated that since TIT did not grant BS degrees, therefore I must start my studies at the junior level. She totally ignored my master's degree from Ohio University, even though both OU and UI were accredited by the same organization. I took a Friday off work and drove to Champaign to argue my case. She was totally unmoved. I also went to see the dean of the graduate school. The dean was also a professor of chemistry and he happened to be Shirley's PhD advisor. He was very sympathetic to my case but since Miss Ham had the absolute authority in foreign student admissions, he could not help me. He did say that I could still keep my assistantship during the first year; after that, it was up to the department. Needless to say, I was totally disappointed and depressed.

After I came home, Nancy was equally disappointed. We talked about what we could do next. I definitely could not go to University of Illinois as a junior. I could always find another job, of course.

A month or so later, while I was running an experiment making a reinforced plastic pipe, Mr. McGinn, the VP in charge of the research division, came by to see me. After we said hello and he watched me work for a while, he told me that the A. O. Smith

Corporation had a program to send one of their promising master's-degree-holding engineers back to graduate school for PhD studies every two years. It had started about five years ago. If I could wait for a year, the company would send me to school. I told him on the spot that that would be great because I enjoyed my work for the A. O. Smith Corporation. He said on the way out he would talk to my lab director, Mr. Ken Charter. While my finished pipe was being cured, I went by Charter's office. Both he and Fred were there. They congratulated me for making a wise decision. I could not wait to get home and tell Nancy the wonderful news.

My problems and troubles were gone. Fred also told me before quitting time that day how the program worked. The person who was sent would be on half-pay and retained their health insurance benefits. The company would also pick up tuition fees, books, and moving expenses. There would not be a written agreement, only a verbal understanding that after two years the person would come back to the company while finishing their dissertation. When the person completed his degree, the company would offer him the market-level salary for that degree, or the person could go out and find a better paying job if desired. I could not believe the company's generosity. When I finally came home and told Nancy about it, we went out to celebrate.

I wrote to the chairman of the aeronautical engineering department at UI, telling him I would not be studying at his department and why. He wrote back to say that he understood. I began thinking about which school to apply to for my PhD studies in 1964. Actually, the choice was quite obvious. The University of Wisconsin-Madison was only seventy-five miles away, and their most respected professor, Gerald Pickett, was once a technical consultant for our plastics research laboratory. Dr. Bodine had been his student. I was accepted into the engineering mechanics PhD program in early 1964.

Chapter XII:

Entering Parenthood

In early November 1962, Nancy fell ill. I took her to see a doctor and we found out that she was pregnant. We were a little bit worried but mostly very excited about the prospect of being parents. The baby was expected in July 1963. Our apartment at the time was on the fourth floor of the building. It would not be convenient or safe for a pregnant woman to climb all those stairs, so we went looking for a different place. We found a one-bedroom apartment in a small, eight-unit, single-story apartment building just south of my work. The company had closed down the lab at the edge of town in 1961 and moved everyone back to the basement of the main building on Twenty-Seventh Street. I could walk to work in less than five minutes. Even as an engineer, I still belonged to the union and had to punch a time clock. I did not have to drive. Nancy would have the car during the day. She could go places, visit the grocery and do other shopping, meet with friends, and so on. She was very happy.

This apartment building had a basement with a sink and drain. For $3 we bought a very primitive "semi-automatic" washing machine. Nancy connected the machine to the water faucet and put the machine's drain pipe over the floor drain during washing. She disconnected and pushed the machine to the side to make room for other tenants to do washing when finished. Since we didn't have a dryer, she had to hang up the laundry to dry. This setup was not that good, but it beat going to a coin-operated laundry.

One day around the end of May, Nancy was getting ready to do some washing in the basement. While she was pushing the washing machine, she felt something in her belly stretch and also felt some wetness. I took her to see her OB/GYN, Dr. E. J. Schmidt. He said her water had broken and she was going to lose all the amniotic fluid. Since the baby was not due for another month, during that month she would need to rest. Without the fluid the baby would have no protection. From that day on she had to rest on the couch or in bed. She could only carefully get up to go to the bathroom.

On June 2, 1963, a Sunday, Wai Fah came to town to visit. I believe he was on his way to New York. I had just gotten dinner ready when Nancy started to have contractions. I called the doctor and he told me to time her contractions. When the contractions were five minutes apart, I was to take her to the hospital. I carefully got her into the car, told Wai Fah to go ahead and eat and to feel at home. I had no idea when I would be back. As I drove down the street toward the Deaconess Hospital, most people were going less than 30 mph.

Figure 8: Nancy and I at the Milwaukee Botanical Gardens three days before Hector's birth.

Finally I got to the emergency entrance and they wheeled Nancy in and told me to go to the counter to fill out some paperwork. I was barely finishing up the last bit of paperwork when the doctor came out, shook my hand, and congratulated me on the birth of our son. He was 4 pounds 12 ounces, and 18½ inches long. The time of his birth was 8:55 PM. Shortly after, I was allowed to see him through the window of the nursery. The nurse showed me a very small baby who had lumps on top of his head, one on each side. His face was very wrinkled. He looked like a baby monkey, but he was beautiful to me. I was not prepared for him to come so soon. I had not picked out his English name yet. We did know his Chinese middle name with Father's help. His middle name would be "Tsung Hwa," meaning his ancestors are Chinese.

I left Nancy and the baby at the hospital to rest and went home since Wai Fah was there. Wai Fah congratulated me for becoming a father and told me that in the last place he visited, his sister had had a baby when he arrived. What a coincidence! I did have a book of names for both boys and girls. I did not want to pick a common name, such as John or James. I went down the list and saw the name Hector. I thought it would be a good one. If he used only his initials when he grew up, his name would be H. T. H. Chen. So I decided his name would be Hector. The next day I went to the hospital and told the nurses his name, so the hospital could put it on his birth certificate. Nancy thought it was fine. Later on when people at work, especially Tao Chiao, heard about the name, they laughed and asked me why I picked that name. I then looked up the name in the dictionary. The verb *hector* means "to bully." I thought to myself that it would be better for him to bully other people (which I could teach him not to do) instead of being bullied. I also found out that it was the name of a Trojan hero. The name is more common among Latinos.

After Wai Fah left, Nancy remained at the hospital due to her slow recovery. After one week the doctor gave the order to discharge her, but Hector had to stay a few more days. Although he was born at 4 pounds 12 ounces, after the nurses dried him, his weight was down to 4 pounds 9 ounces. The doctor wanted to see his weight up to 5 pounds before discharging him. We went to see him in the nursery every evening after dinner and check up on his weight of the day. At the end of the second week after he was born, his weight was up to 4 pounds 15 ounces, we begged the doctor to let him come home. Nancy was crying almost every night after she came home without the baby. The doctor, after carefully checking him, finally agreed that he was a healthy baby who did not have any of the common symptoms of being premature, even though he was born a whole month early.

Before Hector was born Nancy fully intended to breastfeed him, but because of Nancy's weakened state she did not have enough milk to feed him. By the time Hector was released from the hospital the lumps on his head were gone. According to the doctor, it was due to the fact that Nancy had lost all her amniotic fluid. Being upside down, he got those swellings by banging his head on Nancy's pelvis. Our parental tasks began upon his coming home. Due to his small size, he had to be fed eight times a day, around the clock. Since I had to work, we arranged for me to do the 11 PM feeding. Nancy went to bed before 10 and got up at 2 AM to feed him. It would be my turn to get up at 5 in the morning to do the feeding. Then I would have some cereal and go to work. It normally took over an hour to feed and burp him. After he went to sleep for about an hour and a half, it would be feeding time again.

Everyone at the office was very excited about Hector's birth. Because of his low birth weight people always asked me about his weight of the day. To avoid answering everyone's inquiries, I put up a chart on the wall next to my desk tracking his weight and height. A friend lent me a baby scale so Nancy and I could weigh him every evening after we gave him his bath.

During the Christmas holidays of 1963, our little apartment was full of people. David and Gwen, Wai Kai and Shirley, Renee Mah, James (Yao) and Eunice, Wai Fah and Lily (I don't believe they were married yet at the time but Lily was going to school in Illinois and she came along with Shirley and Wai Kai) all came to see the first baby born to our generation. We took apart the double bed, put the mattress and the box spring on the carpeted floor of the bedroom, and all six women slept in there. All five men slept in the living room, mostly on the floor. Hector's crib was stuffed into the shallow closet next to the living room. Hector was happy because he got a lot of attention from everybody.

For this big group of people, the women did the cooking most of the time. Eating out was not considered during those days because of our student budget. We had a great time, catching up on old times, and trading stories about how each of us got to the United States.

I was quite productive at work on top of school (I was taking one class at UWM) and helping Nancy with the baby. I proposed the so-called "Chen Weeping Formula" for the reinforced plastic pipe being developed by the A. O. Smith Corporation based on long-term accumulated testing data, using short-term cyclic pressure tests incorporating interlaminate stresses and glass fiber and resin compositions. I was able to show the correlation between the long and short-term tests. I passed my proposal by another A. O. Smith Corporation consultant, Professor Pi of Marquette University, as he was an expert in fatigue analysis. He was somewhat skeptical, but did not find any faults with my presentation. Fred and I co-authored a paper, "Critical Collapse of Thin Walled Reinforced Plastic Cylinders," which we presented at the eighteenth annual Society of Plastics Industries conference in February 1963, and subsequently published in the proceedings of that conference.

Chapter XIII:

Doctoral Studies at the University Of Wisconsin-Madison

Prior to my formal application to the University of Wisconsin-Madison, I made appointments with Professor G. W. Washa, the chairman of the engineering mechanics department and Professor Obert, the chairman of the mechanical engineering department. I discussed in detail my plans for my doctoral studies with them. I planned to major in engineering mechanics and minor in mechanical engineering since my master's degree was in mechanical engineering and some of the MS credits might be transferable to reduce my course workload. Professor Washa essentially approved my plans verbally. So I filed the official application, put my plans for the study on paper, and planned to start my full-time graduate work in the summer of 1964.

I also applied to the university housing department. Since I already had a child I was given priority for a one-bedroom apartment in Eagle Heights, where most married graduate students lived. The apartment was a spacious one, about the same size as the one we had before. Because my company was paying the moving expenses, we replaced some of the Goodwill furniture with new pieces. We also bought a 1962 Ford Falcon and traded in the 1958 Dodge. We had bought the Dodge by trading in my 1955 Ford. The huge Dodge with tail fins was a disaster, as it had a leaky head gasket. I hoped that the Falcon would last us until I finished graduate school, and it did.

In April, after all the plans were in place, I wrote a lengthy memorandum to Mr. McGinn through our lab director Mr. Charter. I laid out my detailed plan and asked for his approval. His assent was quick and accompanied by a promotion for me. I was promoted to the position of junior scientist with a monthly salary of $800 (an increase of about $40). Since this was the lowest "management" position, I was out of the technical union and no longer required to punch the clock. I did not abuse the privilege. I would go to work a few minutes before or after 7:30 in the morning, and instead of leaving to punch the clock at 4:30 in the afternoon, I usually stayed until 5 or later. I used the extra time to study for school.

In mid-June we moved to Madison. For the next two years I received in the mail a monthly paycheck of $400 less deductions. This amount was almost twice as much as an assistantship paid, came twelve month a year, and required no duties. I even got some profit-sharing checks at Christmas time. Occasionally they would ask me to go back to attend a meeting related to my past work, or share some ideas, but these requests were infrequent.

With Nancy taking care of Hector, I concentrated on my studies without any distractions. Before I moved to Madison, I went to see Professor Gerald Pickett and told him about my study plan and asked him to be my doctoral dissertation advisor, and he agreed. At that time the graduate college required all PhD students to have reading proficiencies in two foreign languages. Although Professor Washa told me a Chinese student managed to get approval for using Chinese as one of the two, Professor Pickett would not agree to that. He suggested that I study both Russian and German. Finally we bargained down to German and French.

As soon as I registered for the summer session, I also registered for a reading short course on German as I had decided the German would be the more difficult language. The short course lasted about eight weeks. There were two reading proficiency tests given during the year. I passed up the winter one, as I need more time to study. The other one was given during the summer. I started the short reading course in French during the next summer (1965), before the German reading exam was given. I made up cards with foreign vocabulary words and put them in my shirt pocket. I studied them as I rode the bus to school. Sometimes, when I heard someone say something on the bus, I thought I understood the meaning of the words but could not distinguish the language it belonged to. I was so confused between English, German, French, and sometimes even Chinese.

When the summer German language exam came, I took it. It was an oral examination. I selected a German text in advance and brought it to the exam. The examiner opened to a random page. I had about fifteen minutes to look over the text and translate it into English verbally. I passed it on the first try, so I did not have to deal with German again. In the summer of 1966, I went to take my reading proficiency exam in French, which followed the same procedure. After I finished with my translation of the page in the French text, the examiner said that he did not know if my weakness was in French or English, but he decided to give me a low pass. I thanked him profusely. To me, a pass is a pass. After he signed my certificate I told him I would not be back again. One of my fellow students took the language test a half dozen times before passing it. A year later, they changed the format into a written multiple-choice test. That student was on his fourth try by then. The school notified him of his latest failure with a postcard, the score written with a red grease pencil. He had gotten a -5 (because he was deducted points for a wrong answer). We all had a good laugh. I don't know when they abolished that language requirement. At least when Hector went to Madison for his PhD twenty years later, he did not have to endure these tests.

During the summers of '64 and '65, Professor Pickett was in India helping one of the universities in Bangalore (I believe) to establish their graduate program. I kept myself busy with course work and thinking about my dissertation project. Before Pickett left for India in the summer of 1965, he suggested that I should do my dissertation in the area of bending of plates with arbitrary shapes and with mixed boundary conditions. He had asked a faculty member in India to do similar work, but the colleague had not made much progress in two years. This research involved quite a bit of computer programming. Since I had never taken a course in computer programming, I attended a short course during the summer, to learn the programming language in a hurry. I never told Professor Pickett that I had no knowledge of computer programming (at the time the language of choice was FORTRAN). I believe computers were introduced into the University of Wisconsin in early 1960. I learned to punch "IBM" cards as both source program and data, and to operate the IBM 1620. We usually signed up in ten-minute intervals, loaded the source deck, and ran the computer in the Engineering Computing Lab. The lab was open around the clock, staffed by graduate assistants majoring in computer science. Once our programs had been debugged we would submit our deck to a bigger and more powerful Control Data machine for more extensive computations. These machines usually ran graduate-student projects over night. One time, based on my own program, I found a basic logic error in the computer. The company who provided the computers agreed with me and fixed it. Professor Pickett was quite pleased with my progress in programming. Sometimes he even asked me to help fellow graduate students with their programs.

I was anxious to get my PhD done in the shortest time possible. During the fall semester of 1964, I submitted my program of study, outlining all the courses I was to take including the transferable ones I had taken at Marquette University and UWM. I also decided to do my minor in physics because I had taken quantum mechanics during the summer and was increasingly interested in physics. Also, with the help of Professor Pickett, I established my PhD supervisory committee: Professors Pickett, Johnson, and Schlack. I took twelve credit hours every semester, except the last one, when I started to do dissertation research.

At the beginning of my studies, I told Nancy that I planned to spend three years on this effort. If I failed important exams, like the qualifier or preliminary, and was disqualified from going forward, I would go back to the A. O. Smith Corporation if they wanted me back. Otherwise I would go find another job. I also promised her that during the week I would spend all my time studying, but every

Sunday afternoon and evening, I would be spending time with the family, no schoolwork. She liked that. I was so happy that I had such an understanding wife. During the summertime, we slept with the bedroom window open (no air conditioning) and we often heard fellow graduate student couples having loud arguments.

Toward the end of 1964, we found out that Nancy was pregnant again. We felt so lucky to have a second baby on the way because Hector was such a delightful child. We were also happy that the company health insurance would cover everything for the whole process. Nancy's OB/GYN, Dr. Carter knew that Hector was born premature, so he warned us that often the second child would be premature too. The previous doctor, Dr. Schmidt, always told Nancy to watch her weight gain. Nancy never gained more than 15 pounds during the entire term with Hector. Dr. Carter did not give such advice, so Nancy gained about 35 pounds during the second pregnancy. The anticipated delivery date was in late August, about then same time Gwen (Gwendyline) was to have her first baby. If the babies were both girls, we decided the first one born would be named Juliana Tsung Li. We did not talk about the names of baby boys. But I looked down the list of the boy's names in my booklet and saw the name "Victor," which also ends in –ctor. This time I was prepared, I told myself.

When we found that Nancy was pregnant again, I put in an application for a two-bedroom apartment right away. My application was approved in the spring and we moved into a first floor two-bedroom apartment with the living room facing a large open grass field. The neighbors across the hall were the Pierces. They had a girl, Elizabeth, about Hector's age, and they played together quite nicely. Steven Pierce, studying for his PhD degree in Physics, was in his sixth year in graduate school and his wife was about to lose her patience. Sometimes she just took off, bringing Elizabeth with her, and went to her parents' home to cool off. When that happened, Nancy usually invited Steve to have dinner with us while his wife was gone. Mrs. Pierce would usually come back within a week. On some Sunday evenings, after putting the kids to bed, we would share a six-pack of beer and play bridge, just to have some kind of social life.

Hector was a healthy and active boy. He ran in and out of our apartment and went to play with Elizabeth all the time. Sometimes he did not even want to come home for dinner. One late July afternoon, as Nancy tried to drag him in to give him his dinner, she felt something strain in her abdomen and a wetness, familiar experiences from when Hector was born. We called Dr. Carter and received instructions to take Nancy to the hospital for observation. I took her to Madison General Hospital. After I completed all the admission paperwork, the doctor told me to go home. He would keep Nancy over night in the hospital for observation. I went home, got Hector from our neighbor—they had watched him while I took Nancy to the hospital—and fed him dinner. About a quarter to eight, the hospital called and told me that we had a boy. Victor was born at 7:31 PM, July 26, 1965, also a month early. But he weighed 6 pounds 1 ounce and was measured at 19 inches long.

Compared to Hector, Victor was a big baby. He did not need to spend extra days in the hospital, even though he was also born a month early. Victor skipped the midnight feeding on the first night he was home, and usually had a bigger appetite. He was also a very healthy baby.

There was a big piece of open land across from our apartment building's parking lot. One day, when some of the wives got together, they talked about what a waste of space this land was. They then went to talk to the university housing department to have the area plowed and leveled. They had it divided into many 10 foot by 10 foot lots, separated by a thin rope for walkways. Those families who wanted to plant something only had to contribute a dollar a season. Nancy was so excited that she got a lot. She planted tomatoes and other Chinese vegetables. Many times when I came home from school near midnight, Nancy would get up from her sleep and stir-fry some Chinese greens for me. I don't know how long that land continued as a garden for the graduate students after we left. We visited Eagle Heights twenty years later (when Hector was in Madison for his graduate studies). The land had been filled up with apartments.

Figure 9: Hector (left) age two years, nine months, and Victor, age eight months.

One day in April 1966, Dr. Blanchard came to visit me. He did that about once or twice a year, as he was monitoring my progress. This time he told me that the company had gone into a partnership with Dow Chemical about a year before and started a manufacturing plant in Little Rock, Arkansas to produce reinforced plastic pipe. The current plastics research laboratory had been downsized to just the chemistry group. Tao Chiao of the chemical engineering group left at about the same time to join Rock Island. As a matter of fact he contacted me to join him at Rock Island and give up my PhD studies. I declined. There would not be a mechanical engineering group at Rock Island. Mr. Pflederer had been transferred to Arkansas. The new company's name was DowSmith Corporation, with Dow Chemical providing the raw materials, resin and glass fibers, and A. O. Smith providing the technology. The new company would not be doing any research. So it did not need a PhD scientist. I was free to pursue my professional career, per our original verbal understanding. In other words, the company would not be offering me a job. He did say that A. O. Smith would be happy to provide me one more year of continuing financial support for my dissertation work on any topic of my choice. He would tell Professor Pickett about the company's decision.

This changed everything. I was preparing to move back to Milwaukee at the end of the summer and continue my dissertation work there. Since this was the last semester of my course work, I would soon free to find a job anywhere, perhaps a teaching job, to finish the dissertation. After Dr. Blanchard left, I went to see Professor Pickett. I told him about my thoughts and asked for his advice. He thought for a moment and said that leaving the campus before the completion of my dissertation would be a bad idea, because there were too many of his former students who left the school too soon. They could never find the time and energy and ended up without a degree. If I was interested in a teaching career, why not start at Madison? I would be among friends, and if I should make any mistakes, I would know where to seek help. I thanked him for the advice and decided to stay for another year. But I wanted to get off the A. O. Smith Corporation's payroll. I went to see Professor Washa about an instructor's position in the department. He received me after I told him my intentions. He pulled an engineering text from the shelf, opened to a random page, and asked me to read aloud to him. After a few minutes he told me to stop. The reason he asked me to read aloud was because there were too many students who complained that foreign instructors' accents were hard to understand. He said he was satisfied that my English was good enough to teach. The department did need people for the next academic year but he wanted to talk to my professors and get their opinions before he would give me a firm offer. In about a week the departmental secretary handed me a letter from Professor Washa offering me a full-time instructorship at $6,800 for the academic year 1966-67. At almost $750 per month, it was a whopping 87 percent increase over my half-pay from A. O. Smith. Nancy was even more excited than I. We would not have to move for a year. She liked the Eagle Heights environment. With fellow graduate students as neighbors, life was very peaceful. By the time we needed to move, Victor would be two and Hector would be over four, much easier than one and three.

Figure 10: Victor (front) and Hector at Eagle Heights, summer 1966.

Toward the end of summer, I sent in my formal resignation to A. O. Smith Corporation, thanked them for their generosity, and informed them that I did not need another year's support from them. Thinking back, I do not feel that I owed them much. I signed over my patent in early April, based on my work on reinforced plastic pipe, to DowSmith. I got a token dollar in return, but the patent would be worth a lot to the company. Although I do not feel I owed the company much, the A. O. Smith Corporation holds a warm place in my heart to this day.

At the beginning of the summer, Professor Pickett went to India again. I talked to him about the general direction of my dissertation work before he left and he seemed to be pleased. While I continued to develop my programming skills I also began to write a draft of my dissertation. For the second time in two years, we took a vacation. I took the family on a sightseeing vacation in northern Wisconsin. I had lived in Wisconsin for six years and never ventured much north of Madison. The first vacation we took was during the spring break of 1965 when we drove to Rochester, New York to visit David and Gwen.

My teaching assignment consisted of three classes of the same subject, Statics and Strength of Materials. It met four times a week, so my teaching load was twelve credit hours but I only needed to prepare my lectures once. This class was mostly for non-engineering mechanics majors. There was another Strength of Materials class which had a two-hour laboratory each week. I would go to the lab to observe the experiments being performed and familiarize myself with the testing machines being used.

My dissertation draft came along nicely during the summer. I wrote a couple of different computer programs to handle different boundary conditions and different shaped plates. I eventually merged them into one general program to handle almost all combinations, and accumulated a lot of data. I also used my program to compare my work with examples in which analytical solutions were available. The correlations were almost 100 percent. By the time Professor Pickett came back and school started in September, I had pretty much had completed a draft.

One day in October, I went to see Professor Pickett and handed him my dissertation draft. He was astonished that I had done so much. He was now obligated to read my draft so we set up appointments, two or three times a week, to go over my work. In about three weeks we went through the whole thing. He offered some minor grammatical corrections and told me to have it typed up. I went to a commercial place where they had the best electric typewriters (no word processors yet) and typists. I had the typing done quickly and made four copies of the dissertation. With Professor Pickett's approval, I picked a date in December to have my oral defense. The day came and I was a little bit nervous. But I told myself no one could know more about my dissertation than myself. So I bravely faced my PhD supervisory committee, Professors Pickett, Young, Johnson, and Schlack. The professor who was supposed to represent the physics department (my minor professor) called me a day earlier to inform me that he would not be there, but if my committee passed me he would sign my certificate of examination too.

Once my presentation started, I became calm and confident. I went through the theory, the methodology, and the use of a computer program—a tool that would become prevalent in the future—to illustrate my contribution to the field of mechanics. The committee had a few questions, but I handled them with ease. Finally it was time for me to step out of the room so the committee could debate my performance. Many of my fellow graduate students, such as Lee Chia-Lee, Neu Xion-Ping, and others, were there outside the examining room to offer moral support. They had all come a year or so earlier for their PhD studies. Since I had come this far in only two and half years, they were very anxious to find out if such a speedy route was feasible. Many students often took a long time, and they tended to blame the faculty, saying that all the professors wanted was to keep the grad students there for cheap labor. Less than twenty minutes later, Professor Pickett opened the door and signaled me to enter. There were smiles on all the examiner's faces. They all came up to congratulate me for a job well done and then left the room. They all had signed my certificate of examination. The day was December 8, 1966 and I had officially earned my PhD. The commencement in January was just a formality.

Figure 11: PhD graduation picture (January 1967) with Hector (left) and Victor.

CHAPTER XIV:

Job Hunting

One advantage of finishing my studies midyear was that I would have plenty of time to find my next job. There was an opportunity to go east during Christmas, as the Bethlehem Steel Company was interviewing for a mechanical engineer. I applied because David and Gwen were living in New Jersey, not far from Bethlehem, Pennsylvania. David was working for the Celanese Corporation at the time. He had finished his PhD studies at the University of Rochester. Bethlehem Steel flew us in. I left Nancy and the kids with David and Gwen and went for the interview. The heavyset chief engineer of Bethlehem leaned way back on his chair, plopped his feet on his desk, and proudly told me that at Bethlehem one got four weeks of vacation after one year and eight weeks of vacation after two years. I made an offhand remark that I was looking for a place to work, not take vacation. He immediately took his feet off the table and sat up in his chair with a straight face. He told me of course I could always work the extra four weeks and the company would pay me additional money. I knew right away that I would not get an offer from Bethlehem Steel. But that did not disturb me.

After a couple months of teaching, I found that I liked it. So I paid a lot of attention to openings from universities. The first such a job I applied to and interviewed for was at McMaster University in Hamilton, Ontario, Canada. It was an overcast January day, cold and damp. It threatened to snow but did not. The university facilities were old and the faculty members who walked around with me during my interview were not particularly cheery. I hoped I would not get an offer from the school, because I did not want to live in a town like Hamilton.

The next interview was in early February with Kansas State University in Manhattan, Kansas. I flew from Madison to Chicago for a connecting flight to Manhattan. The interview with the faculty of mechanical engineering went well and I had an appointment to meet with the dean of the engineering college, Dr. Paul Russell, after lunch. When lunch was over, the professor who was acting as my escort told me that the dean was tied up at the state legislature on budget issues, and the weather report said that it might snow in the early afternoon, so I should go to the airport and see if I could catch an earlier flight. Otherwise, I might be stuck in Manhattan for awhile. I took his advice and caught an earlier flight. Shortly after the plane took off, the captain came on the PA system and told us that he was notified that the Chicago airport had just been closed due to heavy snow. Without further instructions he chose to proceed to Chicago anyway. Soon we were in the Chicago vicinity, and there were many planes in the air. We took up a circling pattern like every one else. We were in the air for more than three hours hoping that Chicago would open soon. In the meantime, I had a small pack of peanuts and an 8-ounce carton of milk to eat, and nothing else. The pilot finally got instructions to land the plane in Kansas City, Missouri. It took three and a half hours to cover about 120 miles. After we landed, the plane barely got off the runway before we came to a full stop. We could go no further. There were planes everywhere. Good thing I only had my attaché case and no other bags for this interview trip. I followed a line of lanterns provided by the airport workers to the terminal. There were people everywhere. I got into a line working its way toward the ticket counter. It was about 9 PM when I reached the counter. I explained to the ticket agent that it was of paramount importance that I get to Madison. She told me there would not be any flights going to Chicago that night, and the only alternative I had was a train leaving for Chicago at 11:30. The airline would issue me a voucher for the train and a voucher for dinner. I quickly took both and went to the airport restaurant. They were about to close up because there was little food left to serve. I got a stale sandwich and a drink. Upon finishing I went outside and waited at curbside. A van came by and took me and others to the train station. At the train station I had time to give Nancy a call to tell her about the situation.

Sitting on a hard wooden bench and being rattled, I did not sleep a wink on the train. Finally the train pulled into Chicago around 9 AM. I managed to catch a train leaving around 9:30 for Madison, and finally arrived in Madison around 12:30 PM. Nancy came to the station, picked me up, and took me directly to school. When I got to my office, my officemate asked me where I had been. There had been a number of students who had come looking for me with questions because I had scheduled an exam for that afternoon.

After the Kansas State University interview experience (in addition to the years in Wisconsin) I told myself that I needed to look for a job someplace much warmer in the winter. At the time I never thought of Arizona. I had never of about the state of Arizona.

The reason I applied to Arizona State University (ASU) was because I saw letters from their engineering mechanics department chair, Dr. C. E. Wallace, posted on the bulletin board outside my departmental office in Madison. I saw his letters in early 1966 and again in 1967. In 1967's letter, he announced that his department had two openings, one in solid mechanics and the other in dynamics and vibrations. I had no idea where Tempe (the home of ASU) was. The skimpy Arizona map that I had only showed the city of Phoenix, not Tempe. Since I had just started my application and interview processes, I decided that I could use the experience. I got an invitation for an interview from Professor Wallace and I headed west two weeks after my Kansas State interview. I did not know what to expect. I arrived in Phoenix after 11 PM. Professor Wallace was there himself to pick me up from the airport and take me to the Sands Motel on Apache Boulevard in Tempe. He told me I could easily walk from the motel to his office in the Engineering Center since the motel was directly across the street from the campus.

The next morning I got up and found it was a bright sunny day, around 70° Fahrenheit. I went across the street and walked toward the Engineering Center on a path (later I learned the path was called Palm Walk) with palm trees on both sides. The interview was pleasant. Most of the faculty members were fairly young and hired in the past five years. After the presentation of my dissertation topic, we even went out for a beer. In the evening, Dr. Wallace came to pick me up for dinner at his home. I met his lovely wife, Teresa. They had only been married a couple of years. I was so overwhelmed that when I went home to the cold snowy weather, I told Nancy that I had found paradise. ASU would be the place we should live and work. I wouldn't even haggle over salary if they offered me a position. Nancy was also happy, just on my descriptions of ASU. About two weeks later, Dr. Wallace called and told me that they had decided to offer me the position of assistant professor. I was so excited that I accepted immediately. He asked me if I wanted to know the salary offer and if I needed to talk with my wife. I told him it did not matter as my wife and I had already discussed moving to Tempe, and both looked forward to working and living there. He sounded so pleased, and told me that my starting academic-year salary would be $11,000. A formal offer letter would be forthcoming. So I had found my next job in March. About a month later, Dr. Wallace informed me that I needed to be on campus a month early to prepare experiments for a laboratory course the college had just started on mechanics of materials for the fall semester. I would be paid an extra month's salary.

Now that I had found a job, I needed to be thinking about the preparations for the move to Arizona. First our family needed a new car. Nancy and I decided on a station wagon. With the boys growing up such a car would be very useful. Also, while I was interviewing I was told how hot the Arizona summers would be. So the new car needed to have factory-installed air conditioning. So we went car shopping. Victor was too young to have an opinion, but Hector picked the color of the car—a burgundy red. Nancy and I decided on an Oldsmobile F-85 with a manual transmission. We visited a couple of the Oldsmobile dealerships, and the minute we mentioned that the car must have factory air, the salesman's eyes lit up. He immediately started rattling off other deluxe equipment that was available. We quickly told him that we only wanted the factory air, not the dealer add-on type, which was a little box hanging on the passenger side. The car otherwise should have standard equipment with a stick shift. Of course none of the dealers had such a car on their lots. So we asked one of them to order one from the factory, at the best price we could negotiate. In early May we received the 1967 burgundy station wagon. It cost less than $2,950 including taxes. We traded in our Ford and paid the balance with a loan from the University of Wisconsin credit union. We had a few thousand dollars saved up, but I needed to preserve cash for a down payment on a house in Arizona and for the move. According to Dr. Wallace it was school policy that ASU did not pay moving expenses.

During the early spring, I received a call from Bernard Harris. who used to be one of my technicians working at A. O. Smith and who went to evening school for a BS degree in mechanical engineering at UW-Milwaukee. It took him more than 10 years to finish. When the plastics research laboratory moved the ME group to Little Rock, Arkansas, Bernie did not want to move his family. He got a job with Rex Chainbelt, Incorporated (it was renamed Rexnord later) as an engineer. His company needed a consultant to help improve the design and manufacturing of their agricultural helical knives, and he had thought of me. I was happy to gain experience in consulting and besides, the extra money couldn't hurt. I drove to Milwaukee one day a week on their project and billed the company $20 per hour. On hot summer days, Bernie's colleagues all squeezed into my wagon to go to lunch. My wagon seated six, and was the only one of our cars that had air conditioning.

I used a simple mathematical model to show how the knives could be made in a more precise way. Nancy even helped me build models to illustrate the idea of using a simplified approach to building machines to speed up production and come up with more precise knives. I suggested that the same concept should be used in knife-sharpening machines. I ended my weekly trips to Milwaukee some time in July, when I had to move to Arizona. I finished my consulting service with Rex Chainbelt in 1968. This was partially because of the distance, and partially because they were a relatively small company had relatively simple products. I didn't have much I could do for them past the initial consultation.

Chapter XV:

Teaching at Arizona State University

According to my road map's mileage chart, it was 1,892 miles between Madison, Wisconsin and Phoenix, Arizona. We planned to spend four nights on the road. That meant I only needed to drive about 400 miles per day. On day one, the children slept quietly and we drove about 750 miles, mostly along Route 66. We arrived in Flagstaff, Arizona around noon on the fourth day. When we stopped to fill the gas tank and to have lunch, the temperature was in the low eighties, which made me wonder if what my future colleagues had told me about hot Arizona summers was true. We continued toward Phoenix and then reached Tempe. We arrived at the same Sands Motel where I stayed during my interview trip around 6 PM. When we opened the car doors, the air hit us like the heat from a raging furnace. We almost couldn't breathe. It was around 110 º. My colleagues did not kid me!

Since I arrived almost a week before I needed to report to ASU to work on the testing laboratory syllabus, I immediately set out to find a house to buy. I picked up a copy of the local newspaper, the Tempe *Daily News*. There were very few advertisements of houses for sale. The day after we arrived, we went to see a house for sale by owner on Balboa Circle about two miles from the campus. It was a small four-bedroom, two-bath house, about 1,750 square feet, on a cul-de-sac. It looked pretty good to us, coming from a two-bedroom apartment. The owner was an associate professor of education and had accepted a position with the University of Arkansas at Little Rock. I tried to talk him down $500 from his asking price of $22,000, but he wouldn't budge. He said he was teaching summer school and had just put the house on the market the day before. He needed to stay in the house until the end of August and he was not in a hurry to sell. On the same day I contacted a realtor, who took us to see two or three houses and promised to show us more the next day. The next day Nancy did not want to see any more houses. The hot weather made her and the kids easily tired. She wanted to swim with the boys in the motel's pool. So I went with the realtor alone. We looked at houses priced from about $18,000 to $25,000 but none could compare to the one on Balboa Circle. On the fourth day we went back to that professor's house on Balboa Circle. I made the offer again and he still wouldn't budge on the price. So we agreed to buy at his full price. I wrote a check for $500 as the earnest money, and he wrote me a receipt on a piece of yellow tablet paper. We agreed to meet at his title company in a couple of days to process the formal purchase contract and to open escrow. At that point I told him that I was totally at his mercy on all procedures involving this transaction since I was a new hire at ASU and this was the first house I had ever bought. He looked into my eyes and said I could totally trust him to play fair. His wife nodded her head in agreement.

At the title company I tried to understand what the escrow officer was talking about: mortgage assumption, VA loan, interest rate, and so on. It turned out all these terms had something to do with how much I was going to pay for the house. First the house had a VA loan of 5.25 percent, which I was qualified to assume if I could come up with the difference between the purchase price and the balance of the loan. I needed to come up with around $3,000 to close the deal. I wrote the check from the bank in Madison, and the title company accepted it because I also showed the escrow officer the letter that offered me the job from ASU. In retrospect I did a lot of stupid things when buying this house, buying from a FSBO (for sale by owner) for one, and not knowing anything about the real estate market for another. I just lucked out because this professor was an honorable man. He did not do any damage to the house after closing, and he even had the carpet cleaned without our asking after he moved out.

Although we had bought a house, we could not move in for another month. I got a call from the moving company that our furniture would be arriving the next day, so I needed to find an apartment for a month in a hurry. We found one nearby and the manager agreed to rent to us for just one month at a slightly higher rent. We checked out of the motel and drove over just as the moving van arrived a day early. We were temporarily settled down. The next day I went to ASU to report to work.

I went to Dr. Wallace's office to report in, and he walked me to the personnel office and left me there to fill out paper work. After lunch he showed me the engineering testing laboratory and we walked to the engineering development shop. Here he introduced me to the shop boss, a Mr. James Heywood, who was a retired navy chief petty officer (I later learned). Heywood treated all the young faculty members with contempt. I eventually earned his respect by showing my knowledge of the laboratory machines and specimens that I required.

The week I arrived at the ASU campus, I got a call from Mrs. Shultz, the department secretary back at the engineering mechanics department in Wisconsin. Professor Pickett had taken ill and had been admitted into the hospital. She told me that a couple days after I left Wisconsin he had a heart attack. He would not be able to attend the Midwestern Mechanics Conference to be held at Colorado State University in Fort Collins, Colorado August 21-23, 1967. I was to go by myself. A technical paper based on my dissertation work had been accepted for presentation at the conference and for publication in the conference proceedings. He and I originally planned to meet at the conference. I was so looking forward to see him there, and ASU had told me that my expenses in traveling to the conference would be covered. A few days later Mrs. Shultz called again and told me that Professor Pickett was recovering well and even talked about going to the Colorado conference. But on the morning of his scheduled discharge from the hospital, he had another heart attack and passed away.

I was extremely saddened by the passing of the only advisor whom I could always go to with my questions and problems. I went on to the conference, and my presentation was scheduled in an afternoon session. There were supposed to be five papers presented and mine was the third scheduled. Before I started, the session moderator, Professor J. R. Goodman, who knew Professor Pickett and considered him a friend, announced the passing of Professor Pickett. He also told the session participants that the last two presenters would not be there. Since Fort Collins was a small town there was no other activities planned for that afternoon except a barbeque picnic after the session. I knew the conference attendees, with all that time on their hands, would ask a lot of questions, so I took my time. My original twenty-minute speech stretched to about forty minutes. Upon finishing, the questions began and I tried to answer in as much detail as I could. Some of the participants started sidetracking into questions I could only admit that I did not know. Fortunately Professor Goodman stepped in and told the conference attendees that he thought I had done a very good job. Upon adjournment of the session, many of the participants came up, shook my hand, and congratulated me for a job well done.

Returning to ASU, I was assigned an office in the Engineering Center "A" Wing on the second floor. I shared it with Dr. Harold D. Nelson. He had arrived just before the fall semester started. Although he was the first PhD graduate from the engineering college of ASU, he had been teaching at Wichita State University for two years while completing his dissertation. ASU started its engineering college in 1955, and the PhD program in the early 1960s. Dr. Lee P. Thompson was the founding dean. Harold was an instructor at ASU while he was working on his degree. Apparently most of the senior professors liked him very well and he already knew all of them. He was promoted to associate professor in two years.

There was another Chinese assistant professor, George Mah, in the engineering mechanics department. He came a year before me. In my third and his fourth year we both were put forward for promotions by the acting department chair, Professor Ted Allen. Dr. Wallace was on a sabbatical leave. Both of us were turned down.

I learned later on that this was due to a general lack of support from the engineering Promotion, Tenure and Retention (PTR) committee for George. Due to the lack of support for George, the PTR committee decided to not grant me the promotion as well. My gut feeling that the lack of support was because George was married to a nice Caucasian woman. Also George was quick to make caustic remarks, usually directed at one or two members of the administration. Although he would never make such remarks to their faces, word must have filtered to them and they all sat on the PTR committee.

George left the following year and got a position at a university in Colorado. I was promoted to associate professor in my fourth year at ASU. In the early 1960s it was not against the law to discriminate. Although the civil rights bill initiated by President Kennedy was signed into law by President Johnson in 1964, most Americans believed it pertained to African-Americans only and did not apply to other races. About a year after I came to ASU, people started to know me and my good nature. As a result I was called all kinds of names, e.g., Chinaman, Odd Job (the Korean who played Goldfinger's henchman in a James Bond movie). I was called such names by at least two of my colleagues to my face. They even made slant-eye faces and made jokes about my karate-chopping them. I put up with this abuse for a few months until one day I could not take it anymore. During a walk to lunch with these colleagues and Professor Ted Allen, they acted up again. I stopped walking and told them I would not go to lunch with them anymore and that their behavior offended me. I turned around and went back to my office. I believed they still went on to their lunch. After lunch Ted came to my office and apologized to me. He should have told them to stop, as the senior professor. A few days later one of the two also came to apologize. He thought he was just having a little fun and did not know it caused me discomfort. The other one just pretended it never happened. I at least stopped them from acting stupid and emotionally hurting me.

During the early years of teaching, I tried to maintain certain standards in the classes I taught. Since Wisconsin was the only place

I had taught before, I tried to compare my students' performances at ASU with those at Wisconsin. I routinely failed about a third of my students. Toward the end of the second year Dr. Wallace came to talk to me. He appeared to be very uncomfortable, and told me that the associate dean in charge of undergraduate programs thought I was too tough on the students, failed too many of them, that I should ease up a little. I told Wallace that I was not being too tough on my students. I tried to do my best, helping them outside the classroom by telling them that my office door was always open. I graded them as I saw fit. If the dean did not like what I was doing, I was still in my probationary period and he could fire me at any time. That was the last time I ever heard from the administration regarding my teaching standards.

However, as years went by, I found my standards have started to drift downward. I failed fewer students, not because the newer crop was any better but due to the "grade inflation" that was occurring nationwide. It would be unfair to subject my students to a higher standard while other universities (even Harvard, for instance) and my own colleagues were giving in to the trend. I remembered a particular case involving a pretty female student, one of my advisees. She was admitted to aerospace engineering with a 4.0 high school GPA. I tried to select her classes for the spring semester of her freshman year. I advised her to sign up for first semester calculus, but she refused. After I took a closer look at her high school transcript, she had never taken any mathematics classes beyond algebra. Her GPA was built on mostly superficial classes, not on mathematics or science. When I insisted that she must quickly take the remedial math classes, such as trigonometry and geometry she started to cry. She did not like math and science classes, as they were too hard for her. I asked her why she wanted to major in aerospace engineering. She said because of her GPA everyone told her that she was so smart she ought to be an astronaut. I never saw her again. She either transferred to liberal arts or dropped out of school. I believe our secondary education system had failed miserably in educating bright young students like her and many others.

During the early years of my teaching career, Dean Thompson frequently reminded us during annual faculty meetings that our primary responsibly was to do as good a job in teaching as we could and do research on our own time. I knew that research and publications were also important, because our promotions and mobility (finding jobs at other universities) depended on publications in reputable journals. On the ninth year (five years after my promotion to associate professor) I was promoted to the rank of professor with a decent raise because I published three journal papers during that year. I was happy and working diligently. During those years I was awarded some small research grants, for example, a grant from the Margaret Goldwater Arthritics Research Foundation. I presented some of my results in a meeting with then-Senator Barry Goldwater. But the funds dried up soon after the senator announced that he was not going to seek re-election.

My disillusionment with teaching began after Dean Thompson retired. The new dean was quite ambitious and he stressed that faculty members must seek grant money to support their research if they wanted to get ahead. One year I spent many evenings and weekends developing two sizable grant proposals on top of my normal teaching loads. One proposal I submitted to the National Science Foundation (NSF), on the subject of joint replacement problems. I even went to visit with an NSF program director. The young and arrogant program director told me to my face that he had never heard of Arizona State University. While he was answering a telephone call in the middle of my visit, I happened to look down in his waste paper basket and there was a copy of my proposal, which he had received just a few days ago. I realized right there that our proposals would never be able to compete with those from more prominent universities. It would be decades before ASU would become known as a research university.

I also soon found out that the dean's strategy was to go out and hire well established researchers from other universities, especially if they could bring their ongoing funded research projects to ASU, to buy greatness in a matter of speaking. They usually only needed to teach one course per semester but were paid at least 50 percent higher salaries than existing faculty members at the same rank. They were the ones who would get almost all the annual merit raises. Not only the deans were driving this. A series of university presidents did the same things. The faculty members hired prior to the early 1980s carried most of the teaching loads with no raises and no promotions on the horizon.

The administration occasionally still mentioned "teaching excellence." They pushed student evaluations of their instructors and used the results to the administration's advantage. One such case was Professor Ahmad Hassan, who held a PhD from the University of Arizona. I was one of the three members on his search committee. He would teach aerodynamics among other subjects for our department, the name of which then was and still is Mechanical and Aerospace Engineering, or MAE. He worked hard on his teaching and also tried to develop his research by writing grant proposals. On his third year, he was voted by a student organization as the professor of the year.

Unfortunately, in the annual PTR committee discussions I distinctly detected the undercurrent that many of the members wanted to get rid of him. When I pointed out his teaching award from the students, someone said something like "What do the students know? He must be an easy grader." I did overhear one senior professor talking about him as being "only" a University of Arizona graduate, and an Egyptian who married a white blond American to boot. I couldn't believe my ears! We were into the 1980s, yet discrimination was still raging. Toward the end of his fourth year, when he got the word that he would not be promoted, he quickly got a job with McDonnell-Douglas (now part of Boeing). The industry recognized his potential while our department didn't.

One of my former classmates from Wisconsin, Dr. Stanley Russell (his doctoral degree was in engineering mechanics and applied mathematics) had also been hired into our department. I had talked him into coming to ASU. He was treated fairly for the first few years. His primary love was teaching math and physics. Later, a dispute developed between our college and the liberal arts college which was settled with our college dean agreeing to no longer teach math and physics so the engineering freshmen would take math and physics classes from the liberal arts college. When this occurred, Stanley felt that he has been rendered a second-class citizen. He soon left and went to work for Motorola's mechanical engineering laboratory. He was much happier as a result.

During one of my father's visits in the early 1980s, I confided to him my disillusionment with teaching, and my plan to leave and pursue an industry position. I had talked to Stanley Russell and his lab had an opening. Father's wise advice convinced me that there would always be unpleasantness in any job I had. He also knew how much I enjoyed teaching and told me that money should not be the determining factor. Besides, as full professor, I was already at the top of my rank and I had tenure. I listened and stayed.

CHAPTER XVI:

Naturalized as an American Citizen

Most Chinese people from mainland China in my generation feel the same as I do: that we are a lost generation. The wars in China started around 1900 and lasted about sixty years. My parents started to move around in their twenties. Even my mother had to come to the United States to live with us in her eighties after she had lived in Taiwan for over forty years. She had no other family there after my father passed away. We have no roots to speak of. Even if I wanted to emulate the author of *Roots*, Alex Haley, by going back to China to find where my ancestors lived, I wouldn't even know where to begin. Even if I found a geographical location to start, I don't believe that there would be anyone around who remembered my ancestors because the Communists did a good job of destroying people's lives and family histories.

During the early years I was in the United States, I had decided that this country in spite of its faults was the one where I wanted to live permanently. I followed the proper procedures and processes, and on November 12, 1968, Nancy and I were both sworn in as citizens of the United States of America.

One of my colleagues, Bill Bickford, threw a great party that evening (a weekday) in our honor at his home in Paradise Valley. That was one of the best parties we ever attended because it held great meaning for us. Bill got drunk that night on Seagram VO. He had a hangover the next morning when he came to school and threw up in the wastepaper basket. I had to dismiss his class for him as he was in no condition to teach. To this day he still can't handle hard liquor. Bill is a good friend.

Since I became a citizen, I have never missed voting in a major election. I am registered as an independent, but over the years I may have voted more with the Republicans than I have with the Democrats. Maybe I am conservative by nature.

Chapter XVII:

Visiting Professorship in Taiwan

In early 1973, my sixth year at ASU, I decided to take my first sabbatical leave. The university, based on one's sabbatical proposal, would normally grant a leave (after six years of service) of up to a year. The purpose of the sabbatical was either more time for research or teaching at a different institution, not just for vacation or profit, according to the rules at the time. I thought about going to one of the well-known universities in the United States. Eventually I decided against the idea.

If Professor Pickett, my Wisconsin PhD advisor, had still been living, I might have chosen to join him for some collaborative research. My decision was to go to Taiwan to teach and catch up on my research in one of the colleges or universities. I had received a good education in Taiwan at very low cost to my family and it had always been on my mind on how I should repay that. This would be my opportunity. Before I had sent out any letters, Nancy, excited about the prospect of going back to Taiwan after over eleven years in the United States, mentioned my plan in one of her letters to her sister Mei Lei. Mei Lei's husband, Dr. Kuang Wei Han, was a captain in the navy in Taiwan at the time, working as a group leader in the Chung Shan Institute of Science and Technology (or CSIST), a research facility for the defense department. My brother-in-law took it upon himself to contact the president (an army major general) of the Chung Cheng Institute of Technology (CCIT). Soon I received a letter from the dean of the CCIT engineering college inviting me to apply for a visiting professorship there. So I applied and accepted their subsequent invitation.

My brother-in-law, who took this quick action, had his own motives. At the time Taiwan was trying to develop a missile program, and desperately needed all kinds of engineers and scientists to help with the program. If I had applied elsewhere it would have been inconvenient for both CSIST and myself if CSIST wanted me to be a consultant. But CCIT was located just a few miles from CSIST.

My appointment as a visiting professor at the Chung Cheng Institute of Technology started in September. For the summer I needed to find some kind of employment. I had been teaching summer sessions in prior years, but this time I wanted a change. It so happened that Dr. Wallace had a letter from a local office manager, Mr. Gerald Nelson, of the FluiDyne Engineering Corporation of Minneapolis, Minnesota, requesting his recommendation of an engineering professor for a design project. Dr. Wallace handed me the letter and asked me to respond directly. Mr. Nelson's office was located in Tempe, about three blocks from the ASU campus. He had a one-man office. His managerial duties were dealing with projects of FluiDyne in the Southwest region including California, Arizona, New Mexico, and Texas. He landed a project in designing pressure vessels from a company in New Mexico, but the headquarters in Minneapolis was too busy to handle the added project so they told him to try to handle it himself locally. Mr. Nelson was a civil engineer by training and did not have time to handle the actual work of a project.

It didn't take me long to complete the calculations needed for the pressure vessel designs, and I took a trip to Minneapolis for the purpose of presenting the results to FluiDyne engineers. I never got the chance to talk about my design. Instead the main office was having a design review meeting for a wind tunnel project. Wind tunnels were FluiDyne's main area of business. As soon as I showed up at the main office, I was asked to sit in on the meeting and participate where I could. I attended the review meeting for three days, and upon my return to Tempe, I was sent a small independent project on some structural design of a part of a wind tunnel. When

I finally completed my work in mid-September I said goodbye to Mr. Nelson and was on my way to Taiwan.

At the time I accepted the visiting professorship at CCIT, I decided that our whole family would go to Taiwan and stay for the entire year. I rented our house on Balboa Circle to my colleague, Dr. Bob Rankine, at below-market rate. He promised to take good care of our house and directly deposit the monthly rent to my bank account. This way I would have no worries while I was gone.

Upon my reporting to CCIT, the dean of engineering and I reviewed their master of science in engineering degree program and decided upon the courses I was to offer in each of the semesters. During the year I taught Theory of Elasticity, Theory of Stability, Theory of Plates and Shells, and Fracture Mechanics. The school normally did not offer these courses due to the lack of professors in these areas. Occasionally they had to ask professors teaching at the National Taiwan University to help out. The big disadvantage about this arrangement was that the professors only showed up before lectures and disappeared right after the lectures were finished because the drivers picked them up and returned them to Taipei after every class meeting.

The dean offered me the same transportation service. Knowing that my parents lived in Taipei and my family stayed with them, the school also offered me a three-bedroom furnished house not far from the campus for me and my family. I did use the house, and normally stayed there two or three nights a week. After the first week of class, I told Father I had decided to buy a used car. Originally I thought about bringing my Oldsmobile station wagon with me but the cost of doing so was prohibitive, though not because of the cost of shipping. It was because the Taiwan government was trying to protect Taiwan's own automotive industry, which was in its infancy. Any autos imported into Taiwan were subject to a 100 percent tariff based on the factory price. I would have been faced with a 100 percent tax if I wanted to sell it in Taiwan or I would have to ship it back to the United States. Buying a car in Taiwan, I could come and go as I pleased. During holidays we as a family could visit places with ease. I bought a small four-door sedan, a six-year old Mitsubishi. I told the dean that I would not be using the college's driver services.

Figure 12: Visit to Yang Ming Shan with (L-R) Victor, Nancy, Mother, Father, Hector, and myself, 1973.

Another reason that I needed my own transportation was that my brother-in-law, Dr. Han, arranged for me to consult for CSIST two afternoons a week. Of course, he would send his company's driver for me. I thought two afternoons per week was a little excessive. I finally bargained it down to only on Tuesday afternoons. For that CSIST would pay me NTD $2,000 a month, or the equivalent of USD $50 (at the time the exchange rate was still NTD $40 to USD $1). I was told by a colleague privately that if I were a Caucasian American they would pay me up to USD $5,000 a month. So I was discriminated against in both countries that I held citizenships. I told Dr. Han that I would do the work for free because what they paid me would only cover the gas expense for my car. He just thanked me for the help. I was told privately by the same colleague that it was Dr. Han's idea not to ask for a higher pay because we were related by marriage.

On the first day of class, there were about fifteen students. Seven were officially registered and the rest just sat in, because the school would rarely have visiting professors from overseas and they didn't want to miss the opportunity for new learning. At the beginning I asked the class if they preferred me to conduct my lectures completely in English. They all agreed, which would be easy for me too. The students would have more opportunity to learn English in the meantime. At the beginning of the second week, the class members obviously had a meeting in my absence and decided that they now wanted me to lecture in Chinese while the writings on the chalkboard should still be in English. I told them that since I always taught in English it would be a little bit trying for me to do it in Chinese. They all agreed to help me where I needed it and seemed to be happy. Since all the students were career army officers, they were reluctant to speak up to a higher-ranking officer, or a professor for that matter. Even though I was a civilian, I found out that the people at the school treated me as having the rank of a colonel. Occasionally when I walked the school grounds, people with ranks of lieutenant colonel or below saluted me. It was obvious that they knew me and I did not know them.

During the second week of class a student, First Lieutenant Ta-Ming Liu, came to see me. He asked me if I would be his master's thesis advisor, and help him to find a suitable topic. I agreed even though I did not know about his academic abilities. I was not overly concerned, since army officers had to pass college-level entrance examinations to be admitted into the degree programs just like in the civilian world. It also so happened that I had a half-finished project on the subject of "extensional vibration of plates" on which I needed someone to help me generate some computational data. It turned out Lt. Liu worked diligently and caught up with the project quickly. During the second semester, when the time came for him to draft his thesis, he proposed that he would write it in English. I told him that he did not possess the level of English to write a technical document yet. It would end up that I would be the one to write it for him. He should draft it in Chinese and I would help to edit it. Later on he told me that he was surprised that I had not forgotten Chinese even though I had spent the last fourteen years in the United States.

My Tuesday afternoons at Chung Shan Institute of Science and Technology were spent assisting a couple of mechanical engineers in finishing some mechanical component designs for use aboard gunboats. I also found out that CSIST's library was very up-to-date. It had most of the current issues of journals in my area. It was big, comfortable, and air-conditioned. The librarians were all college-educated young ladies. They even located an electric typewriter pretty much for my exclusive use in typing up my journal paper drafts. After I had my own car, I no longer needed to rely on military drivers to take me to places, so I spent many afternoons working in that library on my research papers.

One day in late October, Dr. Han asked to meet with me in his office. He presented me with a project. He wanted me to lead a team of engineers on a project involving the vibration analysis of a destroyer-class ship. Taiwan had been trying to develop missile systems. Up to that time (1973) Taiwan had some small success in developing and manufacturing air-to-air missiles, because they were small, light, and short-range. Taiwan needed ship-to-shore and ship-to-air missile systems but the United States would neither sell her nor assist her in obtaining such weapons. Dr. Han had been representing the navy in negotiating with Israel in buying some kind of missile to be installed on the destroyers. The final obstacle was that the navy wanted Israel to guarantee the accuracy of the missiles before Taiwan bought them. Israel wanted Taiwan to supply a vibration analysis of the ship. The alternative was to pay Israeli engineers to do it for a fee, and that would require a year before Israel would issue the guarantee. Dr. Han was under a tight schedule and he also wanted to save the government a big expense.

Dr. Han himself held a PhD from the (United States) Naval Postgraduate School in electric engineering with a specialty in guidance. He would not participate in the work. Instead, he assembled a half-dozen engineers and put us in a big room. For the next month or so I was in that room aside from teaching my classes. At long last we had a report on the vibration analysis written in English (saving the government the task of translation) that I felt pretty good about. As soon as the report was typed and reproduced, Dr. Han was on his way to Israel with it. The purpose of his trip was simply to deliver the report in person. There was no Federal Express, UPS, or other document delivery services available at the time. He told me upon returning that his Israeli counterpart simply told him that they would have the report evaluated and would get back to him. I heard from him sometime in late spring of 1974 that the Israeli missile manufacturer issued the guarantee with no comments about my report. For my efforts, I believe Dr. Han got a commendation from the defense department which helped his later promotion to rear admiral, and I was paid an extra NTD $3,000.

In 1973, Hector was ten and Victor was eight. They were in the Tempe Rural Elementary School finishing the fourth and second grades, respectively. Education has been always of paramount importance in our family. Although the kids had learned some Chinese from Mrs. Eugenia Tu in Tempe, living in Taiwan would be a great opportunity for them to be really immersed in the Chinese educational system. Nancy went to talk with the principal of the elementary school at the Taipei Teacher's School about the boys sitting in on classes at the school. Since they had been in the United States, there would be a big issue in the level of their Chinese understanding. It was agreed that they both would be sitting in on the first grade while undergoing tutoring at home. This made them both uncomfortable because of their physical sizes. However, it was necessary for them to learn the phonetic symbols of the Mandarin pronunciations as well as to increase their Chinese level. The plan was to move both of them to the third grade in the second semester. Unfortunately it turned out that there was no space, so as a result Victor stayed in the first grade while Hector moved to the fourth grade. Since Victor was larger than all the other students, his teacher put him in charge of keeping order in class when the teacher stepped out of the room.

Hector suffered in the fourth grade. He had lots of difficulties keeping up due to his level of written and spoken Chinese. Despite the fact that he was just sitting in, we wanted him to be treated just as one of the students in class, but for many subjects, this was his first experience with them, and in a new language as well. Classes such as Taiwan civics and calligraphy were completely new to him. Often times he came home in tears. However he did manage to not be at the bottom of the class (the class size was around fifty-six) by the end of the year. His most happy events were when he was playing basketball. He was the star of the grade school team (due to his height) and he aced the physical education and math classes.

Upon our return to the United States, they had no problems rejoining Rural Elementary as sixth and fourth graders. Because they were either ahead or even in the math and science classes at the school in Taiwan, there was not that much to catch up on. Their English did have a slight Chinese accent during the first couple of months back in school.

At the end of my visiting year, I wrote a lengthy report to the president of the CCIT, Major General Lu, on my views of the academic level of the school and on ways to improve the education system. Recommendations included hiring more full-time faculty exclusively for the school instead of relying on part-time instructors from other colleges and universities, and requiring the teaching faculty to post their office hours. I did that during the year so that students could come to my office to ask questions and get help. I believe the president took my report seriously. He requested more funding and hired more full-time faculty. He gave a farewell dinner in my honor and invited Father to the dinner also. Father was quite proud of the contributions I made during the year. Another thing that impressed Father was during my stay was that I never mixed English in Chinese conversations at home or during any meetings with public officials or his friends.

Also during my visiting year, I was able to complete three research papers which were subsequently published in various reputable journals in my field. The publications resulted in my promotion to full professor the next year (my ninth at ASU), according to the chair of the PTR committee.

After our return from Taiwan, we decided to get a bigger house. We looked around and found that Suggs Homes was developing in the area south of Baseline Road and east of McClintock Drive, about five miles south of ASU. We picked a four-bedroom, two-bath model on Holbrook Lane. Because the houses were not selling fast, Suggs was very accommodating. Normally the developer would not allow alterations to their basic plans, but Suggs allowed us to enlarge the family room and one of the bedrooms by adding about 50 square Feet. We also converted the linen closet in the laundry room into a half-bath, so the bedroom (our guest bedroom) next to the laundry room would have its own half-bath. We also extended the covered patio to the entire length of the L-shaped house. This way we could put a ping-pong table under the patio. Both of our parents had indicated they would come to visit us in the future and would stay with us for an extended period, not like their brief first visits.

We signed the contract in September and by December the house was ready. We did not want to move during Christmas and managed to delay the move until January of 1975. Our $45,000 mortgage loan was at 9.75 percent, which tripled our monthly mortgage payments. The payments were high, but we were happy.

Figure 13: Christmas 1976 with Hector, Stanley, and Victor in the Holbrook house.

CHAPTER XVIII:

Visiting Professorship in China

After President Nixon normalized relations with mainland China, we resumed communications with our siblings in Hangzhou. We were able to write to mainland China directly, but letters from Taiwan had to come to the United States first. In one of the letters Xiao Hui suggested that we ought to think about visiting China. I wrote back that it would be best if we visited not as tourists but instead had some official function. That way the Chinese government would treat us much better. She took it upon herself to contact someone at the National Zhejiang University (I had attended its junior high for seventh grade and fall semester of eighth grade in 1948-50) about a possible visiting professorship. The head of the mechanical engineering department liked the idea, and a correspondence began. In early 1984, I received an official invitation for a visiting professorship from the university. I could choose the duration of the visit: a short one in the summer, a semester, or a year. Before I replied I wrote to Father about the invitation. Since Father was still a member of the National Assembly and a member of the Kuomintang Party, I asked him to request the permission through the proper channels for such a visit. Although I knew I did not have to do that, I did not want to put him in a difficult position with the Taiwan government. The response from the government was positive.

Nancy and I discussed the potential trip and decided that our whole family should go. I responded back to the head of the mechanical engineering department that I would go for two weeks during the summer (since my sons were in college) and that I wanted to bring my family. Both of my sons were born in the United States and this would be a great opportunity for them to see and know where they came from. He agreed, provided that we took care of the international travel cost and covered some moderate room and board expenses while I was in residence at the university (my wife's portion would be covered by the university). In return the university would sponsor some tours of the country at their expense. I wrote to Xiao Hui that we were going. I also wanted to coordinate a family reunion in Hong Kong (at the time still under the control of the United Kingdom) for the duration of about a week. I told her that she should start to make government requests that she, Xiao Lung, and Xiao Yu and their spouses be allowed to visit Hong Kong for a week at about the time I finished my tour of China. I would let our parents know the time for them to be in Hong Kong. We were to stay at the same hotel for the week of the reunion.

My parents were excited, since they hadn't seen their other children for almost thirty-seven years. This would be a wonderful reunion. They would also be able to meet their other children's spouses for the first time. We were not certain that the reunion in Hong Kong would happen as planned. Hong Kong had a very restrictive policy regarding Chinese visitors. Hong Kong only allowed 150 daily visitors from China, of which seventy-five could only be temporary visitors. China has thirty-five provinces and a dozen big cities directly under central government control. Each political entity would have permission for two visitors to travel to Hong Kong per day (this was the Chinese government's own policy). We put our plan into motion, applying for passports for everyone and getting visas, etc.

My lecture topic would be on reinforced materials. I prepared ten days' worth of lectures with transparencies and slides to fill about two and half hours each day. To make sure that Nancy and the boys would not be bored during my days of lectures, I arranged for them to arrive in Hangzhou a week later than I. That way they would still have plenty of time to visit with my siblings and to see the city before we started touring other parts of China.

The university provided me with a two-room suite in the VIP quarters. We had most of our meals in their dining room. For the first week I lectured in the afternoon . I was always being invited by some provincial officials to have lunch with them before my lecture. The meals were quite sumptuous, and Xiao Hui was at most of the lunches. the meals usually had ten dishes and two kinds of wine. So my afternoon lectures were very uncomfortable. On the days I did not have lunch or dinner engagements, the dining room staff offered me beer during meals but served it at room temperature. I noticed they had a refrigerator in the room so I asked them to chill the beer. They did so for a couple of days, but later on the beer was not cold again. They told me that they turned the refrigerator off to conserve electricity.

At the beginning of my lecture I asked the audience if they would like my lectures in Chinese or English, just like I had during my visit in Taiwan. Once again the audiences voted to have me lecture in English. After two days, two students sitting in the front row of the group came to me to request that I lecture in Chinese because during their college days they studied Russian instead of English. So I switched to Chinese and the whole group seemed to be much happier.

During the last lunch, hosted by the secretary of the provincial Communist party, my sister Xiao Hui was not present. Halfway through lunch the secretary made an excuse and left the lunch early. His underlings stayed and commended my coming to China to bring new knowledge. They strongly hinted that I could help my motherland in the future if I would bring new technologies to them during my professional activities. They even offered to pay for my travel to China if I could bring them new developments. I listened with a heightened sense of alert that they were asking me to do some form of technical espionage. I nodded my head in a non-committal way and said I would see what I could do. Before I left Hangzhou I told Xiao Hui about the conversation and I also emphasized that I could never do anything like that. I also decided that I would not come to China as a visiting scholar in the future. She told me that the next time she had a chance to see the secretary she would protest their tactics. My sister was an elected delegate of a non-Communist organization. The existence of such organizations was to show the outside world that the Communist government did allow some form of democracy for the people. Later, according to my sister, the secretary told her that what the underlings did was without his knowledge and they would be transferred out of his organization—if you can believe that.

At the end of my lectures I was paid 100 yuan renminbi, the equivalent of USD $45.50 at the time. At the sponsorship of Zhejiang University we visited Shanghai, Nanking, Beijing, and Xian. At each city a representative from one of the major universities would be our guide to sightseeing and visiting major attractions. We toured the famous Cheng Huang Shan in Shanghai, the Zhong Shan Ling (Dr. Sun Yat-sen Mausoleum) in Nanking, the Great Wall in Beijing, and the terra cotta soldiers in Xian. My family, especially the boys, thoroughly enjoyed the tour. Before we went to Xian I talked to my sister and found out that their trip to Hong Kong had been approved by the government. The Zhejiang government told her in order for all six of them to travel on the same day to Hong Kong they had to borrow quotas from neighboring provinces and cities because of the two-per-day-per-political-entity rule. Through a family friend our parents had been informed and reservations at a particular hotel in Hong Kong had been made on the day of everyone's scheduled arrival.

After our visit to our last destination, Xian, we took the plane arranged by our Xian guide to Guangzhou. The plane was an old rickety Boeing (I don't even know what kind). I could not close the tray table and had to put my foot against it to keep it shut. When the plane was ascending fog came into the cabin through the overhead luggage rack. When it was descending to land, fog came through the floor. Before taking off, two passengers got on board, but since the plane was full, there were no seats for them. Instead of escorting them off, as would be the case in the United States, the stewardesses gave up their seats for them. The stewardesses ended up sitting on a couple of low footstools. I don't know why they had stools on the plane. They held onto the handle of a refrigerator and a counter edge during takeoff and landing. The refrigerator was an old GE model and I couldn't figure out why they would have such a heavy non-functional item on board. I was especially amused when the stewardesses opened the refrigerator door and hung their coats in it. While in flight, I took out my diary and recorded what I observed in detail, in case we didn't make it to Guangzhou and someone found my diary, at least the world would know why we didn't make it.

After we arrived in Guangzhou (the guide's job ended once we left Xian) we had to find our own way to get to Hong Kong. We decided to take a speedboat (it could travel up to 30 mph like a hydrofoil) instead of the train. So we took a taxi to the boat dock. Since we all had U.S. passports, we did not need visas to enter Hong Kong. After we purchased the tickets and went to the bank to convert most of our Chinese currency back to American dollars, we managed to get into a small store at the dock before noon and spent our remaining renminbis on cookies and various other items before they closed down for their lunch hour.

Finally we arrived in Hong Kong around 4 PM on June 14, 1984. I felt so relieved that we were finally in a place that we had some control over. I felt like a millstone had been lifted from my shoulders. We took a taxi to the designated hotel. We checked into our room but I didn't know my parents' room (or whether they had even arrived) or my siblings' rooms. While I was walking around the hotel corridors and thinking about going to the front desk to check the room numbers, I heard somebody talking in the Hangzhou dialect. I knocked on the door and my little sister Xiao Yu opened the door. Most of them were in the room. After thirty-five years—thirty-seven for our parents—we finally had our long-awaited reunion.

Before we went out for dinner, I gave each of my siblings and their spouses $100 Hong Kong dollars to spend on souvenirs or as they liked. I also told them if they needed more money just to let me know and I would go to the bank to convert more U.S. dollars into HKD. I believe my parents also gave each of them some money. When they crossed the border at Shen Zheng to Hong Kong, the (Chinese) government only allowed each of them to bring $10 HKD and 100 yuan with them. They arrived at Shen Zheng the previous evening. Because of their limited resources they did not check into a hotel. They decided to spend the night in the train station and to take the train in the morning to Kowloon after crossing the border. At that time they had already spent over twenty hours on the train. They put their luggage together and took turns sleeping so nobody could steal it.

Figure 14: Family reunion dinner in Hong Kong, June 19, 1984.

The next week went by in a blur. We went out shopping, checking out the Hong Kong malls (especially my siblings, since they had never seen anything like malls, let alone done any shopping in them). We spent time huddling in someone's hotel room talking about old times, trying to catch up on the lost years or going out to eat, all twelve of us. That week of reunion was the happiest time for my parents' lives. Finally it was time to say goodbye to my siblings. We parted in tears, not knowing when we would be together again.

I had arranged for our family to go with my parents to Taiwan for a week. The main purpose for the Taiwan trip was to introduce Hector to a girl, Jennie Shaw. Jennie is the daughter of Richard Kung Shaw. Richard's younger brother Alex and his wife Ping Yao Shaw had brought Hector's photo to Richard during her trip to Taiwan in the spring, and Ping Yao also brought back Jennie's photo for Hector. They agreed to write to each other after they met, Hector in Chinese and Jennie in English. I was told they corrected each other's letters to help improve their respective language skills.

Upon arriving in Taiwan, I immediately telephoned Richard, and he said he would arrange for both families to get together. We finally met at lunch on the third day after we arrived. I suppose the girl's family did not want to seem anxious. After lunch, Jennie took Hector sightseeing around Taipei. For the next three days they went all over the northern part of Taiwan.

Both families had approved of Hector's courting Jennie quite a while ago because we had known Jennie's grandparents for many years. If anyone disapproved, they wisely kept it to themselves. Jennie's grandfather had been strongly in favor of the courtship since Alex and Ping's wedding, when Hector and Victor helped to cater the event. The elder Mr. Shaw was a cousin (or uncle) of Hsin-Chien Liu (whom I had known since I came to Phoenix in 1967) depending on how one based the relationship. Hsin-Chien's mother was the elder Shaw's aunt, so that made Hsin-Chien his cousin. But the elder Shaw's wife was Hsin-Chien's aunt (his father's younger sister), so that made the elder Mr. Shaw Hsin-Chien's uncle in the Chinese tradition. It has always been rather confusing. Hsin-Chien always addressed Mr. Shaw as Uncle just to be respectful. Over the years when the Shaws visited Phoenix, we played mahjongg and drank XO Cognac together numerous times. Mr. Shaw had known Hector since his teens, but watching Hector and Victor help out at Alex and Ping's wedding cemented his opinion. We had also known Richard and his brothers for many years. One time when Richard came to Arizona we went to Las Vegas with him and Hsin-Chien.

So it was with a great deal of happiness for both families that the young ones developed a genuine fondness for each other. In the next summer (1985), Hector went to Taiwan by himself and spent a couple of weeks there. In the summer of 1986, one year before he left Motorola. Hector again went to Taiwan. Nancy gave him a solitaire diamond ring for him to use as an engagement ring if their relationship developed as he hoped. Jeannie accepted his proposal, so we, including Victor, all hopped on a plane and went to Taiwan for the formal engagement party. It was a very pleasant trip and at the request of Adm. Han (my brother-in-law) I even did some "free" consulting for CSIST.

Figure 15 Hector and Jennie's engagement

Jennie's family, in keeping with Taiwanese tradition ordered many boxes of engagement cookies to be given to friends and relatives to celebrate the event. Hector brought back a few boxes for us too. And the following summer he went there and got married in a civil ceremony. Nancy and I made a special trip to Taiwan for the event but missed the courthouse ceremony. Because of the time constraints there was no time for a big wedding banquet, so we had an intimate dinner just for the families. The decision to have a civil ceremony was intended to ease the process of obtaining a U.S. visa so that a formal wedding could happen in America. Jennie's mother, according to Taiwanese tradition, did not consider them married without a big banquet. So their marriage was not consummated.

Before Hector left Taipei he took Jennie to the U.S. Consulate and made an application for his wife to immigrate to the United States as a permanent resident.

**Figure 16 After civil ceremony in Taiwan,
flanked by their happy grandparents**

In September 1987, Jennie came to Phoenix. Hector had moved Madison to start his graduate studies. She stayed with us, with the exception of a few days before the wedding when she stayed with our next door neighbors, Steve and Cecile Rath. There was not enough room at our own house, with my parents and Hector coming. Nancy immediately started to plan for the big wedding ceremony. We set the date on December 27 so that Hector would be on his winter break from the University of Wisconsin-Madison. He originally was going just for a master's degree. then he decided later to go for a PhD in mechanical engineering. We had plenty of time to prepare and informed all our relatives. We had over seventy people come in from out of town. Jennie's grandparents, her grandmother on her mother's side, and her parents all came from Taiwan. My three siblings (without their spouses, since obtaining visas for them would be difficult) came from Hangzhou. We might have overdone it a little—besides the church ceremony we also had a ceremony, Chinese-style, in a restaurant, the China Doll. We had twenty tables, with ten persons each, of guests for the wedding banquet. I booked twelve rooms in the Sheraton Hotel in Tempe and rented two fifteen-passenger vans for the week to chauffeur overseas relatives around. A good time was had by all, and it was a good chance for another family reunion.

Figure 17: The union of the Chen, Shaw, and Liu families.

Chapter XIX:

Extracurricular Activities

Beside full-time teaching and advising graduate students, I had some outside activities and interests to occupy my remaining time. My teaching and other duties associated with the college or department took up on average forty-five to fifty hours per week. To make time for my outside interests, I would meet my graduate students on evenings and Saturdays, especially those students working full-time in industry.

My outside activities and interests were generally in the areas of consulting and investments. I liked consulting work. My first consulting job with Rex Chainbelt in Milwaukee in early 1967 was quite thought provoking and brought modest financial rewards. Beginning with the second year I was at ASU, local industries started to seek me out to help them with small design problems. Attorneys asked me to be their litigation consultant and expert witness. I did not enjoy working for attorneys as much as with industrial clients. The attorneys had a tendency of calling the night before to help them prepare a case or ignoring me for a long time if a case was postponed. There was one attorney who refused to pay me for my work. I tried not to accept work from attorneys. Off and on I had over a dozen court cases that all had a favorable outcome except one.

My most enjoyable industrial client among many would be FluiDyne Engineering Corporation. As I mentioned earlier, I had a summer job with the company during the summer of 1973 prior to my visiting professorship in Taiwan. In 1975, Mr. Nelson from

FluiDyne called me about a wind tunnel project the company wanted me to consult on.

The wind tunnel was an exciting project. The world's largest wind tunnel, located at Moffett Field, NASA Ames Research Center, Palo Alto, California, was going through a $100 million (in 1975 dollars) renovation. The tunnel had been built in the pre-WWII era. The test section was 40 feet by 80 feet, with a test velocity of 100 nautical miles per hour (nmph). With the advancement of jet aircraft, NASA decided it was time to upgrade the tunnel's test velocity to 300 nmph, and to add another leg, making a test section of 80 feet by 120 feet with a test velocity of 120 nmph. FluiDyne, one of the major companies in the United States that specialized in wind tunnel design and construction, was a sub-contractor to John Blum Architects of San Francisco, the primary contractor.

I was to work on the project for the entire summer. I normally left home Sunday evenings so I could be at the Minneapolis office on Monday mornings and returned to Tempe Friday evenings. During the week I stayed at a motel near the FluiDyne office. This meant I would be gone from my family during the week for ten weeks.

Hector was only twelve and Victor ten. The boys loved swimming. During the summer Nancy and I usually drove them to the ASU swimming pool. Now that I would be away so much I didn't want Nancy to have to drive them daily to ASU, even if it was only five miles each way. We decided that we could afford to build our own pool, so that the boys could go swimming any time they wanted. We contracted with Anthony Pools, picked a shape, and asked them to proportionally enlarge the size of pool to cover most of the backyard. This way I didn't have to take care of so much lawn. The final size was about 40 feet long and 24 feet at its widest. It cost $6,400. We took out a pool loan to pay for it. By the end of the next summer I had made enough money from consulting that we had paid off the pool loan. We had them start the work early so that the pool was ready to use by the beginning of summer.

We had a great time every weekend when I was home. We swam and barbecued. Sometimes we even had company over to enjoy the pool. I don't believe that the boys missed me at all.

Before the arrival of summer 1976, I had second thoughts about weekly commuting to Minneapolis, and it just so happened that the higher-ups at FluiDyne had had the same thoughts. They decided it would be more economical for Mr. Nelson to hire my supporting staff locally namely an engineer and a draftsperson. The engineer who could carry out the details of my calculations and designs and a draftsperson to draw up the blueprints. During the year while I was teaching, I was still needed to interact with the FluiDyne engineers and draftsmen from time to time. After a year they identified a portion of the project, the louver section that directs the airflow around the bends of the 40 by 80 wind tunnel, as my exclusive sub-project. The Minneapolis office was busy with many other tasks and they had confidence that I did not need direction from anyone up there, so my weekly trip was no longer necessary.

As a matter of fact, in order to accommodate my teaching schedules, NASA and FluiDyne engineers held many design review meetings in Tempe. During lunch, we seemed to always end up at Monti's La Casa Vieja near the Tempe Bridge.

My design principle for these huge louvers, a device with movable slats for controlling the flow of air, was based on deflections due to air pressure instead of stress levels. Since it was not acceptable to have horizontal supporting beams in the air stream, the louvers themselves needed to be stiff enough to eliminate deflections exceeding one inch. Each louver was to be 70 feet tall and about 22 feet wide. They were to rotate on massive bearings at the top and bottom controlled by a single hydraulic actuator. The contact line of the louvers was lined with two-inch diameter heavy walled rubber tubes. My calculations indicated the contact line would have up to two inches of deflection between the top and bottom of the louver when rotation was required during mode changes (namely, changing from 40 by 80 to 80 by 120 testing mode).

By the end of summer 1977, when I was pretty much done with my design work on the louvers, I was given another tough assignment: studying the fracture mechanics of the massive fan hub. It really wasn't just a study project. I ended up having to design and justify the thickness of the fan hub that held the twenty-three fan blades. Since NASA engineers were running computer problems using the "finite element" method from another consultant (they never did tell me who that consultant was), I had to use a totally different approach. I developed a theoretical approach. Once I had the equations I could make simple calculations to come up with the hub thickness and predict working stresses, etc.

After I submitted my calculations to the NASA engineers I didn't hear from them for a long time. Then one day they scheduled a review meeting in Tempe. The engineers brought a good foot-thick stack of computer-calculated printouts and dumped it on my desk. They told me that the computer's results did not agree with my results by a wide margin. They asserted that my hub was unreasonably thick. I told them calmly that I had no way of checking the computer printouts but I offered them my mathematical equations and asked them to go through them and tell me where I did wrong. I did not hear from them for about four months. Then one day Mr. Nelson got a phone call and told me that the NASA project manager had told the engineers to abandon their computer work and to accept my results. They were placing orders for the fans with the fan manufacturer (at a cost of $6 million each for the six fans, in 1975 dollars) based on my final design.

In my consulting work with FluiDyne, the question of the authority of my designs was raised because I was not a registered professional engineer. So in 1976 I decided to take the professional examination and become registered. Up to that point I did not think that I needed the registration. For several years I was frequently asked to make up exam questions for the exam. It did not make sense for me to take the exam. However, it was required by law that I stamp the drawings of my design because it was a government project. So I started to study for the professional engineering (P.E.) exam. I did not have much time during the day, so I again used the way I prepared for the study abroad exam given by the Taiwan government. I would go to bed around 10 PM and get up at 1 AM to study. I mostly studied heat transfer and fluid mechanics since I did not teach these subjects. I would work until around 4 AM and then sleep till around 6:30. At age thirty-nine, this plan did not work out as well. Toward the end of each week I was very tired and would sleep for ten hours straight to catch up. But I passed the exam and got my mechanical engineer's P.E. license and stamp.

As if I wasn't busy enough, FluiDyne gave me another NASA design problem. This one involved the Cryogenic Tunnel at the NASA Langley Research Center in Langley, Virginia. The tunnel's normal operating temperature was -320° F. The temperature was achieved by evaporating liquid nitrogen into the tunnel after it had evacuated its air mass. The problem was designing a 60-foot diameter "net" upstream of the fans that drove the super-cooled nitrogen gas. The purpose of the net was to protect the fans from any debris or broken model parts. The net used at the time was subject to frequent damage. Obviously the net was under too much stress and the material, stainless steel, was weak and brittle operating in extremely cool gas. I knew right away that the existing net was too flat. I explained to the NASA engineers that if one imagined a one-dimensional net, for example, a piece of string that was pulled tight, it would break easily when it was subjected to a small force perpendicular to the string, because the stress was inversely proportional to the tangent of the angle (near zero) at the supports. Just go out to the countryside and look at the utility lines. They all have a substantial sag to relieve the tension in the line. The NASA engineers said they understood the theory but how could one produce a two-dimensional sag for the circular net? They tried to produce the sag by laying the net in a horizontal position and putting weights on the net. But the difficulty was that they didn't know how much weight to put on the net and how that weight could be evenly distributed. If the weight was not spread evenly, the net could warp. I thought about the problem for a couple of days and an easy solution came to me: using the temperature itself.

First we needed to change the supporting stainless-steel ring (same material as the net) with an aluminum alloy ring. The thermal coefficients of expansion are quite different between the two materials. Aluminum's coefficient is about twice as high as steel's. We would calculate the required sag to minimize the stress level when the nitrogen wind pressure hit the net. I calculated with a nominal safety factor that the required temperature difference would be about 430 ° F. So we needed to clamp the net to a ring heated to about 110° F (which was an easy job) with the net remaining at room temperature (say, 70° F). After the ring cooled down to room temperature a measurable sag developed toward the direction of the fan, and sag increased as temperature dropped. I never heard back from the Langley people how it turned out, but I hope it worked.

During the summer of 1978, I took about three weeks to go to Taiwan at the government's invitation to participate in the National Reconstruction Seminar. During that time Mr. Owen Lamb of FluiDyne was also there. FluiDyne may have sent him to coincide with my timeframe, because Taiwan's Aerospace Industrial Development Corporation (AIDC) was contemplating building a 4 foot by 4 foot transonic (subsonic, sonic and supersonic) wind tunnel. We went to Taichung and met many times with officials of the AIDC. I suppose one of the advantages for FluiDyne to have me there was that from time to time during the meeting, the military officers talked among themselves in Chinese and Mr. Lamb wouldn't know what was going on. They did not bother to translate their internal discussions for him. I wrote down most of their relevant discussions in my report to FluiDyne. I believed FluiDyne eventually won that project and built it for Taiwan.

By 1980 my consulting work with FluiDyne was winding down. The engineering of the Ames Research Center's wind tunnel project was done and construction was in progress. A year or two later Mr. Nelson left the company and started his own engineering firm. I was asked to help him design air conditioning systems for large homes and industrial buildings.

When Mr. Nelson left FluiDyne, my relation with the company was pretty much terminated. One day in the early 1980's, Mr. Nelson showed me a front-page article about the disaster of the re-modification wind tunnel construction project (written six months after the disaster). The tunnel construction work was completed, but a disaster happened during the first day of the "shakedown" run. With the test section velocity at barely 40 percent of the designed 300 nmph top seed, the louver section ahead of the fan section collapsed. Debris flew to the fans and caused some damage. Neither I nor Mr. Nelson heard anything about the disaster when it happened. The article was written later after a team of investigators concluded that the reason for the collapse was not a design flaw. Toward the completion of the re-modification project, NASA had a new (younger) project manager, also an engineer, in charge. During the construction of the louver section he decided that all the ten-inch wide flange steel beams I specified were "way" overdesigned. The manager told the contractor on the spot to fashion the steel beams by using plywood covered with sheet metal so they still looked like steel. This guy obviously had no idea that I had designed for resisting deflections not stress. His idea was that he could save close to $3 million in construction cost. The investigators estimated the damage cost around $15 million. They also concluded that the original design should have been followed.

In early 1976, when the boys were about eleven and thirteen, Nancy felt she needed more of a challenge at home. Since she had been on and off taking classes at ASU's business college, I encouraged her to look into real estate investment. Using the money saved from my consulting work and some money the Hans, Nancy's sister and brother-in-law, entrusted to us to help them invest, we bought an apartment building in Phoenix. Nancy then decided to take classes to get ready to take the licensure exam. I joined her in taking the exam because I knew I would need to go out with her to show houses as well as negotiate contracts (usually during the evening hours) just to have my peace of mind. We both passed the exam at the same sitting.

Most of our investments, obviously, were in real estate. It all started in early 1969. Dr. John Ratliff, an associate professor of English, came to my office and asked me to participate in a real estate limited partnership that he was organizing. The partnership was to buy a twenty-acre parcel at the southwestern corner of Southern Avenue and Dobson Road, where Banner Hospital is now located. The deal was seller-financed. We would make annual payments, and when the land price went up, we would sell the property and make money. The deal looked good (on his say-so), so I bought a share.

About three years later he sold the land to the buyer to build the hospital. The selling price was only about 60 percent above what we paid but based on my out-of-pocket cost I figured I had doubled my money. Over the next few years I participated in about a half dozen of Ratliff's deals, and in all but one I was able to recover my expenses plus some nominal profits. Arizona was a growing state, and successfully investing in real estate was not that difficult.

So in 1976 we went to some business investment seminars. One was on apartment building investments. We bought a twenty-four-unit apartment building, with a mix of two-bedrooms and one-bedrooms, in Phoenix. We had a fairly low down payment, and with seller financing I figured we would have a negative cash flow of about $200 per month. We decided we could manage that amount since I was grossing over $500 per month in my consulting work.

We also joined a small group of investors, two of whom were my colleagues, in a stake in a company called SEM/TEC Laboratories. The firm was organized by an ASU technician, Mr. Edward Holdsworth, to do electron microscopy work. Our share was one-sixth of the company. During the first year, Nancy volunteered to keep the company's books. Ed rented an office just downstairs from my FluiDyne office.

Nancy managed the apartment building with ease. First we raised the rents to reduce the negative cash flow. She went there almost daily to pick up rents from the resident manager and collect money from the coin-operated washers and driers. In less than a year the apartment building began to generate a small positive cash flow, which was quite exciting to Nancy. She believed she could manage more units, so I started to look for other opportunities. I had been thinking that we could organize limited partnerships ourselves.

Now that we were both licensed real estate agents, we joined with Art Dixon of Dixon Realty. Nancy immediately started to sell houses, and she did pretty well. I started to look around for land or apartments to buy. There was an old apartment building right on the ASU campus. It used to be a motel called the Campus Inn, owned by a physician. I started to negotiate with him, proposing to use seller financing. I needed to put together a limited partnership fast. It so happened that a former student of mine, my very first MS student, Mr. Dick Chiang, had quit his engineering job and gone into real estate investments in San Diego, CA. He came to Tempe to investigate an apartment building near the university which he was thinking of buying. He dropped in to see me. After learning of my interest in organizing limited partnerships, he kindly sent me a copy of his own partnership paper after he returned home. I drafted mine based on his limited partnership document and then had my lawyer look it over, for a mere few hundred dollars instead of thousands. The law on limited partnerships at the time set the number of partners at no more than thirty-six, all known to us. This limited our choices to close friends and relatives. I had no problem finding enough people to invest with us.

Since then we have organized a total of seven limited partnerships, two in apartments and five in undeveloped land. One of the apartment buildings, a fifty-unit one, was given back to the lender in 1991, a most difficult time in real estate. Nancy and I, as the general partners, lost the most because we kept on loaning money to the partnership, hoping the rental market would turn around and it never did. However we made money for our partners on the rest of the limited partnerships.

It took four to eighteen years to liquidate all of our partnerships. By 2005 we were totally out of the partnership business. After I retired from teaching I dabbled in stock market investing. Before I retired I usually dealt with a full-service broker. For twenty years I paid him a lot of commission but did not make much money. After I retired I switched to a discount broker and did my own trading online. I lost about $250,000 during the dot-com bust. The only consolation was that I used the losses to offset my real estate gains. Nancy has not let me forget my losses.

We also went into the restaurant business with partners D. C. Wong and C. L. Lai, who both earned MS degrees in civil engineering from ASU. They were never in my classes but were graders for homework papers. In 1986 Mr. Wong approached Nancy as a real estate agent about buying a restaurant to run on a part-time basis. He was and still is employed by the city of Phoenix.

They thought the restaurant business was an easy money-making business. They both worked two years part time waiting on tables in a fairly successful Chinese restaurant. It was so easy: one bought a restaurant, hired a staff, customers came in, ordered the dishes, you served the dishes as ordered, they ate the food and paid the bill. That just couldn't fail to generate real money, right?

Nancy found them a restaurant in the Fiesta Mall area in Mesa that fronted Southern Avenue, a perfect location. At the time it was a Thai restaurant (about 2,400 square feet in the front) and the same owner also owned a Thai imported goods store in the back. After a little negotiation, the partners bought the restaurant business including the floor space in the back but not the imported goods business. Originally, there was supposed to have been a total of three partners. The third investor was in Taiwan. Before the closing, after Mr. Wong informed the Taiwan partner about the purchase, he was told that the Taiwan partner could not come to the United States to sign the final papers because his father had just been diagnosed with cancer. Talk about panic! Since Mr. Wong had already put down $5,000 as earnest money, he needed the third partner's money to complete the purchase. Mr. Wong approached Nancy to see if we would be interested substituting for his third partner. Nancy always had some kind of romantic feelings about owning a Chinese restaurant. Her perception was pretty much as accurate as Wong's. Everyone was hungry for Chinese food. You threw the doors open, people would come in to fill your restaurant, and you couldn't lose. Besides we had just closed the Campus Inn deal, so we had the money. Mr. Wong also assured Nancy that our involvement would be minimal. So out of a total of seven shares, we had three shares and Wong and Lai had two shares each.

We formed CLW, Inc. and named the restaurant Lotus Inn. I became the chairman, Wong the president, and Lai the vice-president. Nancy, with her business experience, became the secretary and treasurer. Since we bought out both Thai businesses, our restaurant would occupy a total of 4,800 square feet. Lai, being an architect, designed the interior. To fund the interior decorations, we took out a bank loan of $70,000 and used our house as collateral.

The management of the restaurant was divided as follows: Wong would be in charge of the kitchen staff, Lai would be in charge of the wait staff and deal with customers, and Nancy would do the books and also deal with advertising, insurance, and everything else. Indeed, the business was booming the first six months. We hit the top of the curve around Christmas, then gradually it started to taper off. Some of the returning customers started to tell Nancy in hushed tones that our wait staff was untrained (which was Lai's responsibility). One example: when there were ladies at the table, they would serve the men first. They didn't understand English well enough and that resulted in the wrong order being placed, etc. True enough, some of the waiters and waitresses were Lai's in-laws who had just come from Taiwan. But I thought they were working very hard.

Six months into the restaurant business, I was already regretting it. Nancy devoted more than 100 percent of her time to the Lotus Inn. She got to the restaurant before opening and would stay until after closing every day. She totally neglected the apartment side of our business. This wasn't the deal we had signed up for. One day after we closed, with both partners present, I exercised my authority as chairman and ended Nancy's daily involvement. She was to be replaced by Lai's wife, Wendy, with pay (Nancy was unpaid). I knew I would be in the doghouse but I had no choice. Her daily involvement might have helped the business, but by neglecting the management and supervision of the resident managers of our apartments, we risked disaster. I also found myself spending every evening at the restaurant. There was no one home after I finished my classes at 7:45 PM (I believed the assistant chair of the department deliberately scheduled my morning classes at 6:40 AM and the later ones at 6:30 PM). There were unkind remarks among some of the faculty members. During one of the curriculum review committee meetings, the discussion came around to the topic of the engineering science major. We were concerned it was not mission-oriented enough, that if some graduates in that major did not go on to more advanced studies, they might not be able to find suitable jobs. One of the committee members, Dan Jankowski, said such a person could always work in the restaurant. Hector's major was in engineering science. Dick Ditsworth said that Jankowski's remark was not called for.

After a year or so, business slowed down considerably. D. C. still worked diligently in the kitchen, but Lai started to come into the restaurant later and later. Some days he came in just before closing. I talked to D. C. about selling the business but he wouldn't agree to it. To own a restaurant was his lifelong dream. Another year went by and the situation in the restaurant became unbearable, especially the behavior of the chefs. The head chef started to drink on the job. One Saturday day afternoon all the chefs walked out. Later I learned that they had pulled a similar stunt at another restaurant in the past. We decided that we would keep the place open for the evening. Nancy got on the phone and called in a favor to get a chef to come in from another restaurant. Hector came in and got on the phone to cancel all reservations, citing plumbing problems. Victor went into the kitchen to attend the soup pot. D. C. took over cooking some of the simple dishes. The wait staff was instructed to smile and suggest to walk-in dinner guests some simpler items. I tended the bar and made the drinks a little stronger. The guests didn't seem to suspect a thing. Finally closing time came. Everyone was so relieved. We ordered pizzas for the staff. The following week the head chef came into the restaurant. We gave him all of the severance checks for those who had walked out on Saturday. A week later he came to our home and wanted to talk to Nancy about letting him come back to his old job. Wong was wavering, but I said no.

Lai got his cousin to come in as chef. We hired other secondary chefs in the meantime. Lai's performance became worse. One day, he confided to Wong that the reason he did not want to work hard was that Nancy and I had a bigger share and he was afraid that we might swallow his shares. He apparently forgot that we had loaned him money up front to be an part owner in the first place. When D. C. told me what Lai said to him, he also recommended that we sell the restaurant. With everyone having a day job, the business could never be successful. We hired an outside agent to handle the listing instead of doing it ourselves, to avoid the appearance of a conflict of interest. After about three years we were done with restaurants, except as guests.

CHAPTER XX:

Our Children

We couldn't be more proud of our children. They were always delightful, friendly, and hard-working. They both finished high school in three years and graduated in the top 5 percent of their graduating classes of 500-plus students. When Hector started high school at the age of fourteen, he was thinking about getting a part-time job after school. I was able to convince him that the part-time job would cut into his study time and would only earn a pittance. It was much more important for him to devote all his time to school work and other extracurricular activities, such as piano, swimming, etc. To make sure the boys would have some spending money to buy the things they wanted without having to ask us for money, we started them on allowances. We started out at fifty cents a week when they were about four or five. As time went by we slowly increased the amount. We opened savings accounts for them. They would deposit their excess money and red envelope money given to them at New Years or birthdays. Nancy helped keep their passbooks. By the time they finished high school, they each had accumulated thousands of dollars in their respective accounts. However, during the last year of Hector's high school and first year at ASU, he worked at ASU's home football games hawking Coke and peanuts. We did not object, since it only happened a few Saturdays during the fall.

They were quite frugal with their money. One time we took them to the state fair. We bought stuff for them to eat. Then they were eyeing the rides so we gave them $3 each and told them they could use it to take any ride they wanted (around 50 to 75 cents each). Anything left over they got to keep. While we walked around the fair they talked between themselves about which one to take. At the end of the evening they hadn't taken any rides and kept the money.

They studied hard and always finished their homework, sometimes even ahead of due dates. When we moved to our new house on Holbrook Lane in January 1975, Hector was in sixth grade and Victor in the fourth. I remembered how many grade schools I had gone through. I did not have any friends during those years. I wrote to the principal of Rural School to request his permission to allow them to stay in the same school to finish the Spring Semester. We would take care of the transportation problem raised by our move. He granted my request, which made the boys slightly happier, even though they missed the Balboa Circle house and the neighborhood. It took them quite a while before they accepted the fact that the new house was our home.

When Hector was about ten and Victor eight, they indicated some interest in learning the piano. We bought a Baldwin upright piano and they started to take lessons from a Mrs. Engelsman. At the time she was studying for her master's degree in music at ASU. By the time we got back from Taiwan, Hector had forgotten most of the lessons but Victor quickly picked up where he left off. About a year later, Hector decided he was struggling too much with the piano lessons and wanted to stop. We understood that each person had different interests and talents. If he did not enjoy the lessons, then it made no sense to force piano on him.

Victor seemed to enjoy the lessons and made impressive progress. A few years later, Mrs. Engelsman told Victor she had taught all she could teach him and that he should look for a more accomplished pianist to learn from. We approached a professor of piano at ASU, and he gave Victor an audition and asked him if he planned to study piano as a career or just for fun. Victor told him that it was just for his own enjoyment but the professor still decided to take him on as a student. We set it up so that he gave Victor a half-hour lesson each week. After a few months Victor told us that he could not keep up with the practice time required to satisfy the professor. He wanted to stop the lessons and practice at his own pace. We agreed.

Hector decided to attend ASU and major in engineering science. Dr. Wallace was his curriculum advisor. Since he took a year of calculus in high school and passed the advanced placement test, Dr. Wallace started him on second-semester calculus—a five-credit-hour class. Hector started to struggle in just the second week into the class. He worked so hard and spent so much time on the class and still ended up with a C, a grade he was unfamiliar with in his studies. The next year and a half he was just ambitious as ever, taking a full load of eighteen credits, studying all the time. But he did not get the grades he was hoping for. I detected that he was suffering "burn out" syndrome. He needed a break and to do something to bring back his confidence. There was an internship program at Motorola's local office. I recommended for him to apply. If accepted by the company he would be working full-time for six months at the technician level and pay. Then he would come back to ASU to continue his studies.

So at the end of sophomore year, Hector started to work full-time at the Hayden and Eighty-Second Street Motorola plant. He also decided to take one evening class. We provided him with a car so he could drive himself to work and class. He requested that he be allowed to move out of the house and live near ASU to save driving time. He had made the same request a year ago when he turned eighteen and we denied it. Now a year later he was able to support himself so we agreed. To provide him with a stable environment we decided to buy him a new one-bedroom condominium just one block from ASU in a development called, appropriately, University Condos. He stayed there for the next five years, even after he graduated. At the end of the internship period, he aced the evening class and Motorola offered him a part-time job with flexible hours. He resumed taking twelve credit hours of classes. His grades improved and he was much happier. The day he received his BS degree (in May 1985) Motorola promptly offered him an engineer's position with 10 percent higher pay than a typical starting engineer. Hector didn't even need to look for a job.

Figure 18: Hector's graduation, May 1985.
Taken in back yard of Holbrook house.

After working at Motorola as an engineer for about two years, Hector came to me and told me that he was thinking about coming back to ASU and studying for a master's degree. He was interested in the field of engineering mechanics. I told him that doing so at ASU would not be a good idea since I was the one who regularly taught all these courses. Most likely he would be in all of my classes. Besides, he already had one degree from ASU, he ought to go to a different university for his master's degree. I recommended three universities with strong mechanics program for his consideration, Stanford, Cornell, and the University of Wisconsin-Madison. He decided he would go to Wisconsin, since he had been born there. My understanding is that when Hector submitted a letter of resignation, Motorola suggested that he take a leave of absence instead, in case he wanted to come back. He called the company after six months and told them that he would not be going back because he had decided to pursue a PhD. He had saved some money so he didn't even bother to apply for any financial aid to slow him down.

In the fall of 1987, we rented a U-Haul trailer, which was towed by Hector's Mustang GT, which was bought new as his college graduation present. I helped him to move across the country. We found a one-bedroom apartment on University Avenue and moved him in. When he registered for classes, he was shocked to find out that out-of-state tuition and fees took a big bite out of his savings. He also found out that he would not be able to do the MS degree program in one year. During the first day of classes, he was quite discouraged about what to do. His savings might not even last for the first year. When he emerged from a class that first day, the departmental secretary was looking for him. It was the same Mrs. Schultz that was the secretary when I was at Wisconsin. From his class schedules, she knew where to find him. She told him that Professor Kessel, the department chair, wanted to talk to him.

Professor Kessel was surprised that Hector spoke perfect English. Based on his name, the professor had thought Hector was a foreign student. Hector told him that he was born in Wisconsin. Professor Kessel told him that one of the departmental teaching assistantships had been awarded to a foreign student who had not come. If Hector would like the assistantship, he was welcome to have it. With the assistantship he would be refunded the out-of-state tuition and fees, and also would be paid a monthly stipend for teaching. It did not take much effort to convince him. His money problem was over. Sometime during the second semester, Hector called and told me that he liked the university environment and the city of Madison so much that he had decided to stay for PhD studies after the completion of the master's degree. We told him that sounded great and assured him that he would have all of our support, financial and otherwise. He returned during the winter break for his formal wedding, which went well. We were happy for him.

Hector finished his MS degree in mechanics and transferred to the mechanic engineering department to begin his PhD studies. Now that he was married, we were looking forward to becoming grandparents, but it took Hector and Jennie over five years to have their first baby. Victoria Li-Chien was born on April 12, 1993 in Wisconsin. Since I was teaching, Nancy went to Madison to help them to cope with new parenthood. Victoria was the most beautiful baby we've ever seen (maybe we were biased, because she was our first granddaughter). During that summer Hector came back to do an internship at Motorola and he brought Victoria home with him. Jennie came for a brief period, but had to return to Wisconsin because of her job. Without her mother, Victoria was a little insecure and wouldn't sleep by herself. One night I got up around midnight and found Hector laying on the couch in the family room with Victoria laying on his chest while both slept.

On October 23, 1995, Valerie Li-Chi was born, our second grandchild. This happened after Hector graduated and had moved to Oregon to work for Intel. It had been difficult for Jennie to become pregnant. So they really had to plan. Jennie's doctor told her to take her temperature every day during a certain time of the month. When the temperature was right, she would call Hector to come home to "mate." She jokingly said that these were the most unromantic intimate moments.

Valerie was a beautiful baby in a different way. Both girls grew up to be young ladies with good manners, as well as straight-A students. I would give most of the credit for raising them well to Jennie, as Hector was too busy working at Intel. My only regret is that the girls never were given the chance to learn Chinese.

Victor finished the fourth grade at Rural School as planned. He transferred to the brand-new Fuller School at the beginning of the fifth grade. He rode his bicycle to school, which was right in our neighborhood. Victor's progress in piano was quite impressive. He even composed and wrote the school song for Fuller. We were all very proud of him. When he finished grade school at Fuller he went to Connelly, a two-year junior high. He then followed Hector's route and went to Marcos de Niza High School, also close enough to ride his bicycle to it. His curriculum was heavy in science and mathematics classes. He also completed high school in three years with ease. He frequently came to my office on Saturdays and played with the sample components used for joint replacement. He indicated that he would someday want to go to medical school and specialize in joint replacement surgery. I told him that he should study mechanical engineering as his undergraduate major as a fallback in case he did not go to medical school later. I also told him that he should go to the University of Arizona (UA) for his undergraduate study. From my experience, the UA medical admission committee had a bias in favor of UA graduates. I had recommended many ASU graduates with very high GPAs to them, and only a few got accepted. One colleague's son had graduated from our bioengineering program with a 3.60 GPA but was not successful in getting into UA's medical college. He had to go to a private medical school in St. Louis, Missouri, paying through the nose for tuition. If Victor could be admitted into UA, his tuition would only be 25 percent of the regular student rate, another benefit of my employment at ASU.

Victor started his freshman year at UA in the fall of 1982. At my urging he did not skip the regular calculus sequence, even though he had passed the calculus advanced placement test. At the end of the year he was on the engineering dean's list. By placing in the top eleven freshmen from Marcos de Niza attending UA, Victor was awarded a special scholarship and a certificate by the high school. Because UA did not have a pre-med program (even though it had a medical school), Victor kept in mind the medical school requirements for specific course work in addition to the ME curriculum. As a result, he always took summer school classes, except during the summer of 1984 when we went to China on my visiting professorship and also spent a week in Taiwan.

During Victor's freshman year, he stayed in the dormitory near the football stadium. Before the first semester was over, they made him a resident assistant, earning a small monthly stipend. After the New Year, our next-door neighbor, Dr. Ahmad Hassan wanted to buy a new car, so I bought his old Mustang for Victor. Our younger son did not come home often because he either had to catch rides with his friends who lived in the Phoenix area or take the bus. He was thrilled to have his own transportation, especially because he had not even asked for a car.

Toward the end of his freshman year he discussed with us the possibility of moving into an apartment starting his sophomore year. The dorm was too noisy with kids running down the hallway at all hours. It just so happened that my colleague Dr. James Stanley had a daughter who about to start the first year of medical school at the UA and also looking for a place to live. I proposed to him to buy a three-bedroom townhouse together, with each of the kids taking one room and renting out the third. We found a brand-new unit about five miles north of the campus, a three-story building with two bedrooms on the second floor and a big one on the third floor. Victor did not mind having Dr. Stanley's daughter, Becky, take the big room. Everyone was happy. Victor even took it upon himself to rent the other room out and collect rent. In about two years, Becky wanted to move out and Victor wanted to stay, so we bought out Dr. Stanley's share after an appraisal. Victor was now a full-fledged landlord. He had to rent both rooms out. Victor lived in that townhouse for close to eight years until he went to Odessa, Texas for his residency. We then sold it for a small profit, and we shared the proceeds with him so he could make a down payment on a condo in Odessa.

In order to secure an admission to the medical school, Victor thought it wise to develop relationships with people who had anything to do with the medical school. He volunteered about eight hours a week assisting a researcher in the medical school who studied artificial bones. One time he brought home some samples and I analyzed them at ASU's testing lab for strength. He sometimes went to the Pima County coroner's office to help out. During one summer break (between the end of the semester and beginning of summer school) he went to Tempe St. Luke's Hospital to volunteer as an orderly. He always seemed to be able to keep himself busy. By the time he was finishing up his BSME degree he already knew a couple of the medical professors on the admissions committee. Of course, whether or not they knew him was another question.

Victor made his application to the UA College of Medicine in the late fall of 1985. He also applied to Wisconsin, Stanford, and the University of Chicago medical schools. He was informed of his acceptance from the UA medical college during the second mailing, sometime in late February 1986. The UA medical college usually admits eighty-eight students. They send out four mailings, each consisting of twenty-two notifications. With the early knowledge of acceptance, he did not need to go to the rest of his applied schools for personal interviews, which saved a lot of cost in traveling. Besides, the UA medical school was both his and our top choice. From our point of view, it was a savings in tuition and a convenience for him. We decided that we would support him through medical school studies. We wanted to make sure that when he graduated he would have no debt.

Victor's medical school was largely successful, except that he failed General and Systemic Pathology, a ten-credit-hour class. We believed it was due to a visit by a girl from the Chicago area he once met on a plane. She came to visit him during his final exam time so he could not concentrate on his studies. He had to retake the failed class, which set him back a year. But the following semester he aced the class and he also used the additional year to take some extra elective classes. We believed that it made him more prepared for his medical career. Although he felt bad, we told him not to worry about it. The extra year he spent in medical school came from the year he skipped (saved) in high school anyway.

When Victor started his rotations in the third year, he found out that he did not much like the specialty of orthopedic surgery. But the OB/GYN rotation got his interest up, and he eventually decided this would be his calling. Now he has a quite successful practice with four other doctors.

Victor has had his share of car problems. One day while he was going from a meeting in the human behavior clinic (one of his rotation subjects) back to the medical school, he crashed his new Chrysler LeBaron, colliding with an on coming car. The LeBaron was bought new as his college graduation present. Fortunately, nobody was hurt. But his LeBaron was totaled. He called us and we drove two cars down right away and left him with the station wagon. On his next trip home we went car shopping. We bought a two-month old Acura sedan that had only 2,700 miles on it. We only had to pay an extra $1,000 or so more after the insurance company reimbursed us for the insured value of the LeBaron. He liked the

Acura even better than the previous car. We heard from him that while he was in Odessa, he drove the Acura though a flooded street and had to have the engine rebuilt as a result.

Meanwhile, Hector was having his frustrations in his studies. His advisor, Dr. Roxann Engelstad, a young assistant professor, was very ambitious and too busy. She had too many graduate students to advise and usually did not have enough time for Hector. In addition, she even relied on Hector to help his fellow graduate students in their research. On the sixth (and last) year at Wisconsin, he called home and admitted he thought about dropping out of the PhD program. I managed to talk him out of the idea and told him to send some of his writings to me, so I could help him through the analytical part of the dissertation. Finally he calmed down and finished his work. He received his degree in 1995. Because of his research topic, in the area of x-ray lithography, he was promptly hired by Intel to work at their Hillsboro, Oregon campus.

Victor graduated from medical school on May 10, 1991. He did his residency in obstetrics and gynecology at Texas Tech University in Odessa, Texas. We rented a U-Haul and I helped him move to Texas. We found a one-bedroom apartment for the first year. When the townhouse in Tucson was sold Victor bought a townhouse in Odessa. He was hired by the Thomas Davis Medical Center in Tucson in 1995 after he completed his residency. Then Thomas Davis was bought out by Foundation Health. In 1996 Foundation Health sold Thomas Davis to Family Practice Associates (FPA). By 1998 FPA had run the practice into the ground and closed its doors. In September 1998 Victor started to work for the University Medical Center (UMC) at its satellite campus on Alvernon Way. Nine months later, UMC decided to close their obstetrics and gynecology department at that location, so Victor needed to find a different place to practice. He was sick and tired of the constant change in these big corporate-owned medical centers, so he contemplated opening his own practice. His wife, Dr. Sally Jean Vetter, strongly encouraged him. When he asked our opinion we told him that he would have our strong support, financially and otherwise.

Sally, an anesthesiologist, met Victor in the operating room of UMC when Victor was the attending physician and she was in charge of the anesthesia. They did not start dating until the summer of 1997. At that time she was in her fourth year of residency.

Sally, a beautiful, tall (by Chinese standards at about five eight), and mature woman, was someone Victor had been looking for his entire life. Victor brought her home to meet us during the July 4 holiday in 1997. I was involved in the Phoenix Chinese United's Fourth of July Beauty contest and I asked Victor to be one of the judges. Nancy and I immediately liked Sally very much. A few months later, in December, I believe, Victor came home by himself. He told us that he would like to propose to her and asked for our blessing. Of course we gave it right away. Nancy also gave Victor a diamond solitaire ring that my mother had asked Nancy to keep for Victor's use since 1987. We also promised him that we would help him in planning their wedding, should he need us to. However, we also knew by then that Sally had been married before and had two teenage kids. I warned Victor that he would assume the position of a stepfather, which wouldn't be easy. He assured us that her children behaved very nicely toward him and he believed that he could help Sally raise them.

Later on, in a private talk with Sally, I learned that she married at eighteen, right out of high school. After two kids, her husband, a blue-collar worker who never went to college, told her that he wanted to get out of the marriage so he could marry someone else, a co-worker, who would be content to be a stay-at-home wife. Sally wanted to go to college. After the divorce, with custody of her two kids, Sally went to Marquette University in Milwaukee and finished her undergraduate degree in three years. Many times she had to bring her kids with her to class. They would sit quietly in the back of the classroom coloring, etc. She went on to the Medical College of Wisconsin, also in Milwaukee, for her MD degree. She did her residency in Milwaukee and at the University Medical Center in Tucson, where she met Victor during her last year in her residency in anesthesiology. Knowing how hard her life must have been, she not only had our love, but also my highest respect for her efforts toward self improvement.

They were married on May 2, 1998. The marriage ceremony was officiated by Sally's father the Most Rev. Eugene Vetter. Sally was employed by an anesthesiology group at the time. Knowing that Victor starting his own solo practice was not an easy task, she nevertheless encouraged him to go for it and assured him that he would have her full support because she was gainfully employed. So in July 1999 Victor rented an office in a medical building and hung out his shingle. With a wife like that, Victor's practice cannot but be successful. We are so proud of both of them.

Victor's practice, known as Generations Health for Women, now has four other doctors in OB/GYN. Sally, in the meantime, has also organized an anesthesiology group that currently consists of eleven other doctors, and has contracts with the Oro Valley Hospital and the outpatient clinic at the Northwest Hospital in Tucson.

In 2003, there was an opportunity for Victor to build a medical building on a lot just across La Cholla Boulevard from the Northwest Hospital, which was where he did most of his deliveries. We encouraged him to go for it. We sold our rental home at Todd Drive in Tempe, used the proceeds as a down payment, and contracted with the Town West Design Development, Inc. to build a 5,040-square-foot building for Victor's practice, although at the time he had only one associate and his rented office space was only approximately 2,300 square feet. We formed a limited liability company called VSSN, LLC. Since we couldn't find a suitable name for our company, Sally came up with the idea of using the first letters of our first names (Victor, Sally, Stanley, and Nancy, hence VSSN). Victor and Sally own 60 percent and Nancy and I own the remaining 40 percent. The tenant improvements were completed in September 2004and Victor's practice moved in at the end of that month.

Victor and Sally were married in May 1998. We eventually got the good news that their first offspring was on the way in the summer of 2001 after returning from our one-week trip to Taiwan and Singapore. The four of us (Victor, Sally, Nancy, and I) had left the United States on June 22, 2001, and returned home on June 30. We spent about two days in Taiwan, visiting the temple in Hsinchou where my parents-in-law's ashes were interned, and other places near Taipei. Jennie's parents were gracious hosts for a busy two days in Taipei. Although Sally was quite tired most of the time, she did not let it ruin our fun. We left for Singapore on the third day to visit Sally's sister, Christine, and my niece, Melissa. It just so happened that both their husbands had overseas assignments in Singapore at that time.

About a week after we came home, Victor called to tell us the good news that Sally was pregnant. Our third grandchild was expected to be born some time in March 2002. We were already committed to a trip with some friends to visit Thailand in early February. But we would have ample time be back before the baby was born, so we did not make any change to our travel plans. We were flying on Japan Airlines with a stop in Tokyo. At my family doctor's suggestion I went to see my urologist to have him fix a catheter for my trip due to my enlarged prostate. He was afraid that I might have difficulties urinating due to travelling fatigue. On the day of the trip, I had used the catheter for three days already. By the time we got to Los Angeles I felt I had a slight fever. I called the urologist's office and discussed with the nurse (the doctor was never available unless you had an appointment) of the possibility of an infection. She assured me that usually was not a problem. So we pushed on to Tokyo. By the time we arrived at the airport and checked into a hotel (we planned to spend a day in Tokyo) my temperature was way up. Nancy took me (with the hotel's help) to a clinic near the airport. The doctor diagnosed that I had developed urethritis. The Japanese doctor gave me antibiotics and IV fluids, fitted me with a gallon-size bag with a catheter, and told me to go home as soon as possible to see my own urologist. Again with the help of the hotel personnel, we were on the plane back to the United States the next day. So much for the Thailand trip …

As soon as we got back home, Victor told us that Sally's delivery date had been moved up a month. The baby was to be delivered by caesarean section because the fetus was not growing properly inside her. I was scheduled to be operated on in the later part of the month. In the meantime my urologist fitted me with a small bag taped to my thigh with another catheter. He did not want to operate on me until my urethritis had cleared up. We went to Tucson on February 6, 2002, the day Sally was to have the C-section. Samuel Li-Jian was born at 4 pounds 5 ounces, seventeen inches long. He was so skinny and had difficulty holding his body temperature. The hospital put him under a warming light. Samuel had to stay in the hospital for several more weeks, being fed around the clock, until his weight increased.

To this day, Samuel, or Sam, is still very thin. Due to his premature birth, he also has (according to Victor and Sally) a pinhole on the wall between two heart chambers. Hopefully it will close by itself when he grows up. He is a very active boy.

Chapter XXI:

Retiring From Teaching

I had been contemplating retirement from teaching for many years. Primarily it was due to drastic changes in the nature of university teaching. In the late 1960s and early 1970s, we were constantly reminded that we must devote our time and energy to doing a good job in teaching. Our students were always to come first and we were to pursue our research and scholarly work on our own time. As time went on, deans changed and we were told to pursue funded research. We were supposed to go after big research grants that would pay up to 55 percent overhead over the direct expenditure to the university. We were supposed to attract graduate students by supporting them financially. In the meantime, quality of teaching was not as important and only a small percentage of the state-supplied budget was used in the teaching area. The administrators were pushing to convert ASU into a so-called "research university" using the existing resources. The college then went out to hire faculty members from other universities that already had funded research grants at big salaries and small teaching loads.

Back in 1987, when Father was here attending Hector's wedding, I asked his advice about my doing something other than teaching, same question we had discussed during his visits in the early 1980's . I had several options, for example, working for Motorola, or opening my own engineering consulting firm or my own real estate brokerage firm, etc. He pointed out that in any line of work there would always be problems or frustrations. I had been teaching for over twenty years, so I must have been doing a good job. I was well liked by my students. I should not just throw teaching away. I seriously considered his words and decided not to change anything or add pressure to our lives. So I continued teaching.

In 1992 the Arizona state legislature passed a law which changed the rules governing the retirement of state employees with full pension benefits. The law lowered an index made up of an employee's age plus the number of years employed by the state of Arizona from eighty-five to eighty without discount for full pension. The amount of pension at the time of retirement was calculated at 2 percent multiplied by the average of three highest years of annual salary out of the immediate five years prior to retirement times the number of years of service.

This was the law I had been waiting for. I started at ASU in 1967 at the age of thirty. By the summer of 1992 I had put in twenty-five years of service. After a serious discussion with Nancy, I wrote a letter to the dean of engineering via my department chairperson and informed them that I was officially retiring at the end of the summer. However, at the request of my department chair, I stayed and taught part time since no one could take over the Advanced Mechanics of Materials class, which was a required course for graduating seniors. I was the one who developed the syllabus and had been teaching it for several years after Dr. James Avery retired and subsequently passed away.

I had been preparing for a job change or early retirement for quite a long time. During the late 1970s and early 1980s, while Nancy was very active in her real estate work, I started a savings plan with a variable annuity life insurance company (VALIC). With Nancy's earnings, I sheltered (tax-deferred) half of my monthly pay each month for almost ten years and cumulated over $200,000 in the account. Meanwhile we continued paying into our limited partnerships our shares for those that were not paid up. We also bought two rental homes using the rental incomes to amortize the mortgages. So when I decided to retire early and not find another job, I knew I could draw down the VALIC account to supplement my monthly income.

Another major reason that I made the decision to retire without second thoughts was that Father passed away in January 1991. Mother could not live in Taiwan by herself so she came to live permanently with us. Nancy was already under a lot of pressure due to the downturn of the real estate business. Mother's constant presence and comments about everything we did added a lot more pressure on Nancy. So I had to retire to keep Mother company and shoulder some of the pressure on Nancy.

Just as I planned, when I was done with my part-time teaching in May 1993, I started to draw against my tax-deferred VALIC account at $20,000 a year. Plus some extra income from consulting and real estate commissions, I was receiving nearly the equivalent of my full-time ASU pay in retirement. I also anticipated that when I turned sixty-two I could start to draw Social Security benefits. With Nancy a year and a half behind me, our income would actually rise.

During the first few months, when I did not need to get up to go to work, I did feel a little bit lost and even a little guilty. Most of my life, I was always busy. I never had enough time to do all the things that were demanded of me or that I took upon myself. Now I had time on my hands that was not spent productively. Sometimes I just sat at my desk, stared out the window, and thought about the money lost on my unproductive empty hours.

When I wasn't busy consulting, I gradually took over some of Nancy's duties in real estate, which she appreciated. I started to list and promote some of our partnership properties beginning in 1994. However, due to too many resolution trust corporation (RTC) properties that came out of failed savings and loan institutions, land values were drastically depressed. We foreclosed on a thirty-acre property (Greenfield Land Company) four years after we sold. We also renegotiated the carrying interest rate, amortization schedule, and pay-off at a big discount on the Lindsay-40 limited partnership. During the Lindsay-40 negotiations, we bluffed that we would walk away from the property (of course the majority of our partners did not agree with that). I calculated that we had saved our partners over $400,000 in carrying cost. This was the biggest poker game I had ever played and won.

In 1995 I was approached by board members of the Chinese-American Professionals Association of Arizona (CAPAA). Dr. Steve Yang, Dr. Tina Liu, and others asked my permission to be nominated for membership on the 1996 board of directors. I agreed, since I was present at the very first organizational meeting of CAPAA back in 1981. Because of a lack of free time, I had always declined to be "drafted" in the past. Now since I was retired from working, it was time I served. As soon as I was elected to the board of directors, I was subsequently elected as the 1996 president by the board during the first meeting.

The 1996 board of directors consisted of Dr. Jenn-Yun Tein, vice-president; Douglas Hum, secretary; Michael Ho, treasurer; and Tina Liu, Jeanette Quong, and D. C. Wong as directors. It turned out that except for D. C. Wong (my former student and a partner in the restaurant business we co-owned) I found new friends among my fellow board members and other CAPAA members. CAPAA grew to 121 paying members. We had nine major activities, usually with an attendance exceeding 150. During August, CAPAA sponsored the Chinese Youth Goodwill Mission from Taiwan, who put on a performance in Phoenix. There were around 800 people that came to see their performance.

In 1997, I was re-elected president, with D. C. Wong as vice-president and Jeannette as secretary. Michael was treasurer again. Drs. Jong-I Mou and Richard Tu replaced Drs. Jenn-Yun Tein and Tina Liu. Since CAPAA was a member organization of the Greater Phoenix Chinese United Association (GPCUA), formerly known as the Phoenix Chinese United Association, I represented CAPAA on the GPCUA executive committee. I was elected the second vice-president of GPCUA in 1996, and then elected its first vice-president in 1997 with the delightful Lani Wo as its president. I led a sub-committee and rewrote the GPCUA bylaws. My revisions were reviewed and accepted, then voted on and passed at the general annual meeting. I quickly withdrew from all activities of GPCUA toward the end of Lani's term, because I knew they would have elected me president of the organization for 1998. This would have taken more of my time and come with a lot of frustrations, since a large number of the members speak Cantonese, and I don't speak or understand Cantonese. Besides, many of the organizations that formed the GPCUA, fifteen in all, were family organizations. They mainly only looked out for their own interests and usually disrupted the proceedings of regular meetings of GPCUA. On top of all that, Mother was complaining that I was spending too much time with these "unproductive" activities and that I shouldn't be so involved.

The real estate market improved drastically starting in 2003. I started to get calls regarding my partnership land listings. We sold the Tonopah-160 limited partnership's 160 acres and closed before Christmas 2004. During the negotiations with various parties on different deals, I was almost tricked into a deal by one "potential buyer" that would have locked up our land for two years at no additional profit to our partners while the "potential buyer" could make a lot of money by "flipping" our land. I was very careful during our negotiations, so I never did sign that proposed contract. That "potential buyer" was quite upset after he found out we had sold the land to someone else. He complained to my broker and demanded commission on his "contract." I told my broker to just ignore him. If he pestered us persistently I would go to the Arizona Department of Real Estate to register a complaint about him, since the potential buyer himself was also a broker.

We sold and closed the Lindsay-40 property at a good profit in early 2005 as well as the Vicksburg limited partnership property in October. During the early negotiations (by letters of intent) on the Vicksburg property, the buyer offered full listing price for our land (at the time I thought I was overpricing it). In the part of the letter indicating who should pay the commission of the sale, the buyer inadvertently replaced the word "Seller" with "Buyer." In the listing I had indicated that we, as seller, would pay the 6 percent commission, to be divided equally between the agents for both the seller and buyer. In the buyer's effort to emphasize the point of who would pay the commission, he made a typo. Of course, I doubted if the buyer himself had actually read his letter of intent (contract) carefully. It must have been his lawyer's secretary who mistyped, and the lawyer had not carefully read it. The salesperson (broker) either didn't read the letter or didn't read it very carefully. At a selling price of $2 million, 6 percent would cost the buyer an additional $120,000. I noticed that at closing the buyer cut his agent's commission by 1 percent, or $20,000.

Nancy and I felt good when the Vicksburg limited partnership deal closed and all funds disbursed. This was the last of the partnerships we had organized back some eighteen years earlier. In between, the real estate market had been up and down at least twice. We sold this land in a up cycle.

We anticipated that we would eventually move to Tucson to be closer to Victor and Sally. Because of their medical practices, they would not likely be moving away from Tucson. Using the funds from the land sales we bought a five-bedroom 3,100-square-foot house plus a lot, both in the Oro Valley area. A few months later, Victor sold his house for a good price, during the housing up cycle. He and Sally wanted to build a house in the Oro Valley area to shorten their respective commutes. They bought the lot from us because they liked the location and size of the lot. We bought it back later from them, because their planned dream house was too big for the lot. We also rented the house we bought to Victor and Sally while they were waiting to have their house designed and built. At the time of this writing they have changed their minds and decided instead to purchase an existing home with a very large backyard that will give the children plenty of room to play. They have decided to keep the lot for now. Who knows what the future will hold?

Chapter XXII:

Mother Joining Us Permanently

My parents had visited the United States many times since their initial visit in 1968. When both Nancy and I became American citizens in November of that year, I asked Father if he would like for me to apply for permanent resident status for him and Mother. At first he agreed but after I started the process, he changed his mind. He was not quite sixty at the time. He was still young and healthy. He was a member of the National Assembly and the chairman of the Finance and Taxation Committee. He could not serve well if he lived permanently overseas. He would have had to make annual trips back to Taiwan to attend to his duties. Other reasons were more practical. He did not speak English and didn't know how to drive, although he could learn. But what would he do to pass the time before mastering the language? With the three of us, namely, David, Shirley and myself, all married and just starting our careers and raising our families, Mother and Father felt they would become a burden to us. I had to agree with him. It would be easier for them to come and visit us every few years, whenever they felt like making the trip.

By the late 1980s, the political landscape in Taiwan had changed dramatically. The old Kuomintang Party had lost the support of the population and the Democratic Progressive Party (DPP) had grown popular among the younger demographic. The indications were that the next president after Lee Tung Hui would come from the DPP.

In 1988 Father finally decided to come to the United States to live with us. He had undergone colon cancer surgery and was recovering well. I made the application for them to immigrate to the United States. It was quickly approved. They came in early 1989 and lived with us. After a few months, after they felt comfortable and were settled in, Father decided to go back to Taiwan to dispose of his properties there. I applied to the INS and got a white paper, which would allow them to be absent from the United States for up to two years. In late 1990, while in Taiwan, Father's cancer returned. Malignant cells spread to other organs, particularly into the lungs. After a short hospital stay, he passed away on January 29, 1991 at the age of eighty-two. We all went back to Taiwan for the funeral. Since my classes were in session, I returned, leaving Nancy with Mother to help handle all the details in winding down the household affairs. I entrusted our cousin, Yuan Shan (Wilson) Chu, to rent their house out for the time being.

In March, Mother returned to the United States with Nancy and brought Father's ashes in an urn. She also brought a spare urn for herself. I purchased two niches at the Greenwood Memory Lawn cemetery in Phoenix. With Victor's help I interned Father's ashes and put Mother's unsealed urn in the niche next to Father's. The internment ceremony was in May. David, Shirley, and the grandchildren all came for the ceremony. Greenwood has close to one hundred years of history, and over half of it is covered with tall trees. It was a very nice and beautiful setting for Father's burial. Victor and I both agreed that Greenwood Memory Lawn was the best among over half a dozen potential sites we had viewed.

Mother started to settle in and became a permanent member of our household. She had her own room and bath, and in a few months she began to be invited to play mahjongg with some of the elders in the community. Many times I had to be the fourth when they were short a player. It was not enjoyable for me to be sitting across from her to play, because she didn't think I was a good enough player and would criticize my play in front of the other two players, whomever they might be.

Mother was never close to any of her children, not even Shirley, the only one among all six of us whom she raised herself. Even though Shirley had lived most of her life up to the age of twenty-one with

Mother (except during 1949 and 1950 when we were by ourselves in Hangzhou), we felt that Mother was no closer to her than any of us. In my own situation, after I was born, I was separated from Mother for eight years during the Sino-Japanese War. During the years between 1945 and 1949, we were always moving and traveling, and were together as a family only three out of the five years. Life did calm down after we got to Taiwan in 1951. But then we were busy studying and only got to see her at supper time, since I usually left for school before she got up and brought lunch to school with what the maid prepared for me. Shortly after I started my studies at the Taipei Institute of Technology, Mother started to play mahjongg, although she often claimed that she did not start to learn the game until after she turned fifty. During those days when there were mahjongg games, we usually ate after the guests (the players) were done eating, meaning even less face time with our parents.

The last eighteen years have been the longest period of time that Mother and I have been together. Yet during all this time, I do not feel that we are any closer. She thinks that Arizona is her home, and that when she goes to visit David or Shirley, she is a guest in their homes. On the other hand, when she is here she either criticizes things Nancy and I have done or is so polite to us that she feels like a guest. She has opinions and comments on everything Nancy does, especially regarding meal preparation. For example, when Nancy prepares a noodle dish, she takes a position right next to the stove and then she will say there is too much water or not enough, too much noodles for the three of us or not enough. It was never the right amount of either. She did that almost every day and on almost every dish Nancy prepared, which drove Nancy up the wall.

Obviously the thought never crossed Mother's mind that Nancy and I had been married and lived by ourselves for over forty years. This was the way she prepared meals and we had survived. I had to explain to Nancy that for the last half century in Taiwan, Mother always had a maid that she could comment and criticize. Over forty-plus years, she has had four or five maids, yet the dishes the maids prepared would always taste the same after a few months on the job. However, at the same time, Mother admitted that she didn't know how to cook. This part was true enough. The few times I challenged her to prepare a dish that she liked, it just did not taste right. It was either too salty or not salted enough, over- or undercooked. So Nancy never asked or allowed Mother to cook.

During the first few years after she joined us, whenever a visitor that she knew from the past came to visit, she always went through her standard routine that she did not really want to leave Taiwan, and that we had forced her to come. She stated that she would rather return to Taiwan and rehire the maid who had worked for her for about twenty years (until the maid retired). She would tell the visitor all these things right in front of Nancy. After this had occurred a few times, I told her not to do that because it made Nancy extremely uncomfortable, and because people might get the idea that Mother was being mistreated by us. She just said that she didn't mean anything by it, but she really missed life in Taiwan. I had to remind her that there were no relatives left in Taiwan, and Father wasn't there. If anything should happen to her, even if I hopped on a plane right away, it would take over twenty-four hours to reach her.

At other times, she seemed so miserable and thought that she wanted to live in a retirement home (some mahjongg player told her the name and location of such a place) by herself. She was under the impression that people lived there and played mahjongg everyday. So one morning I took her to the Hong Ning House on the west side of Phoenix. We looked around the apartment building and the community "living" room and did not see a soul. Finally we talked to the manager, a Cantonese lady, who spoke some Mandarin. After Mother found out that there was no dining room or nurse's station on the premises, she was very anxious to leave. In the car she told me in no uncertain terms that she absolutely could not live there. This "retirement" home was simply an apartment complex that had an elderly Chinese population. For at least a couple of years after that she did not talk about wanting to live by herself in a retirement home.

My brother-in-law Wai Kai told me a similar story about his mother. Wai Kai has five other siblings in the United States. His mother takes turns living with each of them, six months at a time. She grew unhappy and wanted to live by herself in a retirement home. Every time she mentioned it, Wai Kai tried very hard to talk her out of the idea, until one day he decided to bring her to visit one of those places. He took her to the best such place, where many Chinese old folks lived in San Francisco. When their car pulled to the front of the apartment building, his mother wouldn't get out of the car and started to cry. She accused him of trying to get rid of her. For the next few years she stopped mentioning that idea, just like my mother. Mother sometimes told me that I should have let her live by herself a long time ago.

During the first ten years, Mother visited Shirley in Chicago twice and David in Wilmington once. Each time she only stayed there for a few weeks. Otherwise she lived with us and we could not travel anywhere for vacations or take days off. Later, Shirley moved to Fremont, California. During a visit to the Hsuans (old friends of our parents since the Shanghai days), Mother decided she liked it in Fremont because there were many opportunities for her to play mahjongg. In 2004 both Shirley and David convinced her that she ought to pay visits to them at least once a year, since they are her children too. We divided up the year so that Mother would stay with us from late December till May, go to David's (during his summer vacation) for about three months, and then come back for a few weeks. She would then go to Shirley's home from late August or early September till late December. The schedule was interrupted in 2007 because David's son-in-law, Bob Bass, was diagnosed with amyloidosis that affected his heart. Bob had been in and out of the hospital many times. Recently he had a heart transplant and David needed to be on standby, in case his daughter Julie, Bob's wife, needed him. Mother did not go to David's house during the summer of 2007.

After she came to live with us, Mother took two international trips. She went to Hangzhou in May 1992 for about a month. David accompanied her on the trip. This was the first and only time she returned to Hangzhou after she left in 1947. They divided their time between staying with Xiao Hui and Xiao Yu. That was also the very second time in Xiao Lung's memory, first time was the week of family reunion in Hong Kong in 1984, that he met his birth mother. Upon her return from China, Mother decided that that one trip was enough. Xiao Hui and Xiao Yu's apartments were on the fifth and sixth floors, respectively, and buildings with six floors or less were not allowed to have elevators, by the government's decree.

In March 1995, Mother decided to visit Taiwan. Since she was already eighty-four, she might not make it again if she waited too much longer. So Nancy, Mother, and I made the trip to Taipei. We stayed in our cousin Yuan Shan's roomy apartment. Although we only stayed there for two weeks, Mother went to play several games of mahjongg with her old friends.

Prior to our trip, I had a routine check-up by my primary physician, Dr. Englund. He informed me that I was a diabetic. He put me through the typical screening test for diabetes. This meant he made me drink a bottle of god-awful sugary liquid and checked my blood sugar level every half hour for the next two hours. Since my blood sugar levels came down extremely slowly, he prescribed some medicine for me to take. Many times I would get the shakes after I took the pill (my blood sugar was too low). I had to suck on a candy until the shaky feeling went away.

One day, while we were in Taiwan, one of Mother's old maids, Ah Ying, came to visit and brought a big bundle of meat dumplings. The dumplings were made with sweet rice, stuffed with pork and hardboiled salted duck-egg yolks, wrapped in large bamboo leaves. We had them for breakfast the next morning. Since Mother didn't like the egg yolk, she gave it to me and I ate it. By afternoon I had a fever and started to vomit. I stopped taking my diabetes medicine, and in the evening I felt so miserable Nancy walked me to a hospital nearby. The young doctor there diagnosed me as having food poisoning. He advised me to stay on rice soup for a day or two and stop taking the diabetic medicine. When we came back to our cousin's apartment and told Mother about what the doctor said, she simply refused to believe I had food poisoning from the duck egg in the dumpling. So they continued to have the dumplings for breakfast.

A couple of days later, we went to a lunch party in a restaurant. Yuan Shan sat next to me on my left, and during the third dish I happened to glance at him. His face was as white as a sheet. Suddenly he rolled up his eyes and fell to the left. I quickly grabbed his right arm but could not prevent him from falling to the floor. After we got him off the floor, he threw up all over the place. After we got back to his apartment my cousin's wife also said she did not feel so good. At this point Mother had to agree that maybe the duck egg was the cause of all the problems. She had not eaten even one bite. After a supper of rice soup, Nancy and I took the rest of the dumplings and threw them into a dumpster on the street corner.

There was a silver lining in all this, after I came back from Taiwan and told my doctor about the incident of food poison, he agreed that I didn't need to take the diabetic medicine to lower my daily blood glucose numbers. My doctor let the hemoglobin A1c determine my need. Over fourteen years, my hemoglobin A1c level slowly climbed, despite my careful eating regimen (namely, no carbohydrates and mostly vegetables). My doctor put me on 5 milligrams of glipizide daily. After two months my blood sugar came down drastically. Obviously the medication worked.

Toward the end of 2008 and into 2009, my mother experienced several episodes of shortness of breath that resulted in a number of hospital stays. She was diagnosed with congestive heart disease that resulted in low oxygen levels in her blood. We believed that this condition had been developing for a number of years, but Mother had steadfastly refused to submit to any heart checks or invasive procedures. Her opinion was that even if a heart problem was diagnosed, what would it matter? As a result, once the diagnosis had finally been made, her heart efficiency was down to around 25 percent of normal. To make her as comfortable as possible and still allow her to travel around town to play mahjongg, we obtained several portable oxygen bottles as well as a compressor for home use.

At the end of August 2009, Mother experienced another episode of shortness of breath that required a hospital stay. We drove her to the hospital and were fortunate enough to find that the night-duty nurse spoke Chinese. Mother was very happy about the Chinese-speaking nurse and told us to go home, as she felt that we would be back to pick her up the next morning. At around 2 AM on September 1, Mother quietly passed away in her sleep. She was three months shy of her ninety-eighth birthday. A memorial service was held on September 5, and was well attended by family and friends. Mother was interred next to Father in the urn that she had brought to the United States.

Figure 19: Mother and Father's final resting place.

Figure 20: Goodbye, Mother.

CHAPTER XXIII:

Retirement Years and Reflecting on our Lives

Six months after I retired, Nancy decided she would let her real estate sales license become inactive. I agreed to take over anything related to real estate. Until the late 1990s, the real estate market was relatively calm. Property values started to recover only after mid-decade.

My community involvement with CAPAA and GPCUA was limited to between 1996 and 1998, as I mentioned before. I was glad that I was able to make contributions to these two organizations during those years. I also believe that my quick withdrawal from all the Chinese community activities to focus more on the real estate business was the correct move.

We also were able to join a China tour organized by Gwen in 1998 after Victor's wedding. This was the first trip to China since 1984. The trip took twenty-one days, visiting Shanghai, Nanjing, Beijing, Xian, Kunming, Kweilin, Guangzhou, and Hong Kong. It was a very enjoyable trip and we visited many places that we had never been to before. Since then we have taken other trips abroad, mostly cruises, whenever the opportunity arises.

In late October 2007 my TIT graduating class (of 1957) held a fifty-year reunion in Taipei. Over thirty classmates who attended. It was a very memorable occasion. We also took two days to tour around Taiwan and held a meeting with the top administration officials of the since-renamed National Taipei University of Technology (NTUT).

During our reunion we also voted to establish a scholarship at NTUT in the name of our graduating class for good students facing financial hardship. The scholarship will be administered by the university.

I have a wonderful marriage to Nancy, my lifelong companion and love, and we've become closer as we age. We have always made decisions together, big or small. We have two wonderful sons, very accomplished, with wonderful wives. They have given us four beautiful and smart grandchildren.

Looking back I don't believe I would want anything in my life changed. Many times it was life that made choices or challenges for me. All I did was face them and try to do the best I could.